At Home In The World:
The Peace Corps Story

Peace Corps acknowledges the special efforts of Penny Anderson, Janet Getchell, John Coyne, Ron Keeney, and Rose Green in the selection, editing, design, and production of this book.

For more information about the Peace Corps, please call 800-424-8580

Library of Congress Catalog
No. 96-67834

ISBN 0-9644472-1-5

April 1996

CONTENTS

The Spirit of Service

by Mark D. Gearan

Woodrow Wilson once argued that "There is no cause half so sacred as the cause of a people. There is no idea so uplifting as the idea of the service of humanity."

When President John Kennedy established the Peace Corps in 1961, he captured the essence of Wilson's observation. For the Peace Corps was both a cause and an idea: it was a completely new way for Americans to think about public service. The Peace Corps would not be just another government aid program. It would, instead, call for Americans to serve their country by living and working with ordinary people in the developing world, creating opportunities for advancement at the grass-roots level, and strengthening the ties of friendship and mutual understanding around the world.

The Peace Corps' mission is to promote world peace and friendship by:

Providing Volunteers who contribute to the social and economic development of interested countries;

Promoting a better understanding of Americans among the people whom Volunteers serve;

Strengthening Americans' understanding about the world and its peoples.

Peace Corps Volunteers would achieve these goals by living at the level of those they served, learning the local language, eating the same foods, and adapting to the culture of their host communities.

Today, Peace Corps Volunteers are accomplishing these goals and much more. The Peace Corps has become one of America's great success stories, and stands as an example of how the power of an idea and the commitment to a cause can influence the lives of countless people. The men and women who serve as Volunteers embody the spirit of service that is so much a part of the American character, and they are a strong symbol of our country's commitment to the developing world. More than 140,000 Americans have served as Volunteers in 130 countries since the Peace Corps was created. Today, almost 7,000 Volunteers are serving in 94 countries in Africa, Asia and the Pacific, Central and South America, the Caribbean, Eastern and Central Europe, Central Asia, and the Mediterranean. They come from every age and background, and they reflect the rich diversity of our country. Some are fresh out of college; others are people in their in 30s, 40s, and 50s who want to do something different and meaningful mid-way through their careers.

The work that Peace Corps Volunteers do is often basic but always important; sometimes it is life-saving. Volunteers have taught English, math, and science to hundreds of thousands of children and adults around the world. They have brought new farming techniques to rural communities, enabling farmers to grow more food and expand their incomes. Volunteers have immunized tens of thousands of children against diseases and parasites and have helped communities around the world purify water supplies. They have been on the front lines in the successful international efforts to eradicate Guinea worm and prevent the spread of HIV/AIDS.

In recent years, Peace Corps Volunteers have taught small business management and investment strategies. They have promoted entrepreneurial skills to help create new economic opportunities for communities around the world, including the new emerging democracies of Eastern Europe and the former Soviet Union. Peace Corps Volunteers are helping local communities protect and restore their environment after years of neglect. They are also working with local governments to address the social and economic challenges associated with rapid urbanization.

While the responsibilities are diverse, every Peace Corps Volunteer's job has one common trait: it is hard work that requires self-motivation, determination, patience, sacrifice, and a good sense of humor. There are moments of great frustration as well as achievement. Periods of loneliness can accompany the joy of making friendships that last a lifetime. The ability of Peace Corps Volunteers to overcome these personal and professional challenges, however, is what makes them such special people and so successful overseas.

There is perhaps no other government agency that has earned more respect and support from Americans across the political spectrum than the Peace Corps. Ten years ago, on the occasion of the Peace Corps' silver anniversary, President Ronald Reagan had these words to say about Peace Corps Volunteers: "They have conveyed the message that America's heart is large and generous. They have been good neighbors to the people of the world."

The Peace Corps remains a cause and an idea, and Volunteers represent some of the best that America can offer the world. Here at home, they are a source of pride and admiration for their service to our country. Overseas, they are a source of hope and inspiration for people seeking a better future for themselves and their communities.

Mark D. Gearan is the 14th Director of the Peace Corps.

FORWARD

Peace Corps ... More Than You Can Imagine

by Patricia W. Garamendi

Thirty-five years ago, the first Peace Corps Volunteers stepped off a Pan Am Clipper in Accra, Ghana and sang in Twi that new nation's national anthem.

It was a Peace Corps tour de force that delighted the waiting delegation of Ghanaian dignitaries, who had never heard so many Americans speaking their language. When these first fifty Volunteers of the new Peace Corps finished singing, Kenneth Baer delivered a brief speech in Twi, saying that the Peace Corps Volunteers had come to learn as well as to teach.

This statement—we have come to learn as well as to teach—has been a central part of the Peace Corps message all of these years. I cannot begin to tell you how much I learned in two years as a Peace Corps Volunteer in Ethiopia. These lessons are still available for you. Peace Corps is a great education, perhaps the best graduate school America has ever had.

To young people just starting out in life, Peace Corps offers a chance to take a giant step forward. Volunteers who join in mid-career have an opportunity to learn new skills, a new language, and discover what more they are capable of achieving. And to those who have finished one career, the Peace Corps is a new lease on life.

The Peace Corps experience, however, is more than a nice addition to someone's resume. It is a great adventure. It is a moment when you take control of your life and turn it in a new, unfathomed direction. It is the opportunity, as Robert Frost wrote, for you to take the road less traveled.

Nelson Mandela explained why he learned Afrikaans, the language of his prison guards in South Africa: "If you talk to a man in a language he understands, that goes to his head. If you talk to him in his own language, that goes to his heart."

That's what Peace Corps Volunteers do. They speak the language of the people with whom they work. They become part of the communities in which they live. And in doing this, Volunteers give hundreds of thousands of people the belief that they can succeed, that there is reason to hope.

At times we are tempted to think—especially those of us who have been in the developing world—that hope is the most fragile of emotions. The hard facts of life in these nations often attack the notion that anyone might have hope.

But Peace Corps Volunteers carry with them a firm belief that life can be better, that there is hope for everyone in the world. And they share that vision with the people they serve. That is the real success of the Peace Corps. "We have come to learn as well as to teach," said Kenneth Baer thirty-five years ago on the tarmac of the Accra airstrip. We are still coming to learn, to teach, to show that we care.

We did not all have the same job or the same experiences in the Peace Corps. As Volunteers, we have spanned more than three decades and lived and worked in thousands of cities, towns, and villages. However, we all had the same sense of service, the same sense of adventure. Some of the stories told by former Volunteers are collected in this book of essays. These tales are true, touching, funny and, in many ways, awe-inspiring.

Andrew Scott Berman, for example, who served in Togo, describes how he saved the life of a child who had slipped into a river with mouth-to-mouth resuscitation, a skill he had learned during Peace Corps training. Andrew happened to be on the riverbank that day because he had taken his students to the water's edge to teach them a practical lesson in trigonometry.

Susan Rosenfeld, a Volunteer in Senegal, writes about facing, for the first time in her life, a classroom of students in the small coastal fishing town of Joal.

And Orin Hargraves remembers the moment in El Hageb, Morocco, when he realized he had been accepted by his neighbor as more than the strange American who lived upstairs.

Also in the book are essays by Volunteers who have returned to their Peace Corps site years after their tour of duty.

Maureen Orth served in Columbia in the mid-sixties. She returned thirty-years later to where, as a community development Volunteer, she helped build a school now named in her honor. Maureen writes about what it meant to be back in her Peace Corps country. "As I turned to go I realized that at least once in my life, when I was young, enthusiastic and just doing my job, I actually accomplished something that my country and my family could be proud of. And twice in my life, the Peace Corps and the people of Colombia had given me more than I could have ever imagined."

The Peace Corps is much more than you can imagine. Read these essays and you'll see that for all Volunteers, Peace Corps service is a way of being at home in the world.

Patricia W. Garamendi (Ethiopia 1966-68) is the Peace Corps' Associate Director for Volunteer Recruitment & Selection.

The Peace Corps is going to take a lot of people by surprise. It is going to prove that the American revolution is on the move again. When our young people go to live and work in foreign countries, in villages and schools in the developing nations of the world, and put their hands and their skills to work, they are going to make a real contribution, I believe, to world peace. Economic growth in these nations is one of the conditions of peace. Better understanding among people is one of the conditions of peace. Peace Corps Volunteers will contribute to both.

Robert Sargent Shriver, Jr.
March 6, 1961
Peace Corps Director
1961-1966

Ecuador, South America

The Student Arrives at the Door

by Moritz Thomsen (Ecuador 1965-67)

I got my Peace Corps application at the post office in Red Bluff, California, put it on the kitchen table, and walked around it for ten days without touching it, as though it were primed to detonate, trying to convince myself that for a forty-eight-year-old farmer the idea of Peace Corps service was impractical and foolhardy.

I had read that a Peace Corps Volunteer would live at the level of the people with whom he worked, and that they would be poor. Well, I could do that; I had been living poor for years. I had read that the Peace Corps was desperate for agricultural people. Good. That's all I knew. I had raised pigs, corn, alfalfa, beans, and pasture, had laid out orchards, leveled land, and put in wells. And I liked farming. I liked being outside; rows of growing corn, cattle grazing on green pastures, the dusty excitement of a grain harvest—these things were like music to me.

Finally, I filled out the application and sent it to Washington. I was accepted. Sargent Shriver wanted me to go to Ecuador.

Our group, Heifer 3, the third group trained for service in Ecuador—twenty-four agricultural specialists, as we were laughingly referred to—left New York from Kennedy International Airport one midnight and awoke about eight hours later as we landed on the Quito landing strip. Five minutes before disembarking we were all struck with terror, not because of any hardships we might be walking into but because we knew that as part of the welcoming ceremony we were expected to sing as a group the Ecuadorian national anthem.

We were met by a bunch of sweet 4-H Club kids who welcomed us with incomprehensible speeches and great bunches of slightly wilted flowers. We also were greeted by all the Peace Corps brass, some semi-high government officials from the Ecuadorian Department of Agriculture, and the old group of Volunteers who had arrived from all parts of the country to look us over.

Then we huddled together like a bunch of sheep about to be slaughtered, took a deep breath, and swung into the Ecuadorian national anthem. Actually we knew the words much better than the Ecuadorians, whose lips we were trying to read. We were magnificent, rolling out the emotion, swelling in volume, gasping for breath in the ten-thousand-foot altitude. Halfway through the song we discovered with a feeling of exultant relief that the Ecuadorians were trying to read *our* lips.

Before being assigned to a permanent site, we were each sent to live in the village of an experienced Volunteer for two weeks. Our permanent sites remained a secret, not, I think, through any desire to confuse us, but simply because no one knew yet where to put us. I was delivered over to a Volunteer named Byron Bahl, a twenty-three-year-old fellow from Lake City, Iowa, who had been working for the last year in Cariamanga, a town of about five thousand people near the Peruvian border.

I spent the next ten days with Byron in his border town. I followed him around as he worked in the village and in the small rural centers in the hills, where the farmers gathered at the church or in a classroom on the days when they were to meet with the agricultural extension people. We inoculated pigs against cholera, introduced new types of vegetables in community gardens, and Byron gave talks on sanitation and animal nutrition. We visited small farms and a boys' club on the rocky slopes above Cariamanga. There we showed the farmers how to delouse pigs with old crankcase oil and how to treat sick baby pigs with penicillin. We hauled some bags of coffee out of one mountain valley for a farmer who had neither a wagon nor a horse.

In the background of all these activities, the small boys of the town followed us in crowds, chattering and kidding. The girls, who were too shy or too well-bred, stood in the doorways of their houses chanting Byron's name, *"Meester, Meester Byron, Meester By-ron,"* as we passed.

I guess the most touching event was when we delivered the two feeder pigs that Byron had picked up from our Heifer Project organization in Quito for a group of farmers who lived about ten miles outside of town. Months before the pigs were delivered, the group had been coached in a series of weekly meetings on the necessity of a balanced diet and a warm place for the pigs to live. The farmers had organized a pig club and had agreed to build a proper shed. They had done a good job, much too good a job, I thought, constructing a two-room building with five-foot-high walls and an outside pen, all of it of adobe and tile and plastered with cement. It had a cement feeder and a cement waterer, and it must have been built at considerable sacrifice.

We drove out one morning with the extension agent in his jeep, the pigs tied in gunny sacks with just their heads sticking out, both of them furious at this latest indignity. About forty families were waiting for us at the pigpen. It was not a town but simply an open place on the slope of a mountain—a one-room schoolhouse, a football field slanting away toward the valley floor ten miles below, a couple of farmhouses, and a small cabin where the schoolteacher lived.

Wow, what excitement! What exclamations of disbelief as we dumped the pigs into their new home. Eighty-pound pigs at four months? It was incredible; they were as heavy as year-and-a-half-old native pigs, their backs were broad, and there was meat on the hams. They were the first decent animals these people had ever seen, and owning them now, the people lost their cool. Actually, they didn't own them yet. The two pigs were being loaned to the members of the community. The farmers had agreed to feed them properly and care for them according to rules set up by Byron; they were to be paid for by replacing pigs of equal value after the gilt had farrowed. These new pigs in turn would be loaned to another group or another farmer under the same conditions.

My ten days with Byron, ten days in another world, were altogether fantastic, but I wasn't sorry to leave; it was his town, not mine. I was more uncertain than ever of my own role, but in spite of that more anxious than ever to get assigned to a site and start working on my own. There was also a sadness in this cold mountain country that depressed me; early-morning fogs lay fat and heavy in the dry valleys below us, and the thin-soiled rocky slopes, sub-marginal at best, gave no promise of production, no matter what was done to change agricultural techniques.

Early one morning Byron left me at the bus station. "So long," he said. "I've taught you everything I know. Now go on out and save Ecuador." He was a good kid, but he was enveloped in the sadness that brooded over that dark country. As I waited for the bus to leave I suddenly realized with a stab of panic that for the first time there was no one sitting next to me who could interpret my needs to the restless natives; now I was going to have to start learning Spanish.

I thought about the story told of a Peace Corps Trainee who had come to Training the year before and who had learned the first sentence in the Spanish book: "The student arrives at the door, " *Los alumnos llegan a la puerta.*" He went around all day repeating *"Los alumnos llegan a la puerta"* in answer to all questions put to him. We laughed at this story, but it was uneasy laughter because by the end of our first week of Training, we were all saying stunted things as well in Spanish.

Now I sat there in the crowded bus rolling verbs around in my mouth. An Ecuadorian farmer sitting next to me said something; I didn't want to be rude, so I did the best I could. *"Los alumnos llegan a la puerta,"* I told him, smiling. He looked at me, puzzled by my reply. *"Los alumnos llegan a la puerta,"* I said again.

He grinned, then laughed and said something totally incomprehensible.

I shook my head. Well, I thought, it's a beginning.

After five years of watching, I am ready to conclude that young people who "defer" or "break" their careers to serve in the Peace Corps, defer little and break less. Rather they enrich their lives beyond measure, and return better prepared to meet, or better, to originate, adult responsibilities.

Jack Vaughn
Peace Corps Director
1966-1969

Togo, West Africa

Life, Death, and Trigonometry

by Andrew Scott Berman (Togo 1967-69)

everend Father at the Catholic high school was a bit hesitant about giving me permission. But in the end he relented and said I could take my math classes from the boys' school and the girls' school out of the classroom.

Take trigonometry out of the textbook and take it to the field! It was a startling notion, particularly for the French-based, rigorous but dry approach to high school mathematics. In Lama-Kara, Togo that Saturday morning, we met in the center of the village, with our protractors, pencils, sine/cosine/tangent tables and a length of string. For a couple of hours, we measured every shadow in sight and, using principles of geometry and trigonometry, predicted the height of the object. Once we had the shadow to height established, my students marveled their friends and relatives by predicting the height of every flagpole, every house, every person we could find. *Triangles semblables* (similar triangles) they shouted.

Then the finale: the Kara River!

How accurately could we predict the width of the river without crossing it? It was noontime, with not much in the way of shadows. What could we do with mere sticks and string and crude protractors? But mighty trigonometry was at our side!

And so, with a dozen women washing clothes in the river, with another dozen infants playing nearby, we formed a right triangle and enlisted the powers of Pythagoras. The generational leap could not have been more stark: The women washing clothes were living lives as their forebears had for many generations. The students, their own sons and daughters, nieces and nephews, many the first generation to go to secondary school, were using mathematics to solve an engineering problem. Challenges and possibilities were open to them that their parents could not imagine. Explaining who I was to his father, one student introduced me as his *professeur du soleil et la lune* (the teacher of the sun and the moon), since the word "mathematics" did not exist in Cotocoli, the indigenous language that his father spoke.

It went well, with a few hitches. Sine and cosine won't work unless your triangle is really a right triangle. We sighted a tree just across the river. We drew an imaginary triangle using two points along our bank of the river. One point was just across from the tree. There we set our 90-degree angle. From another point on the same bank we sighted the tree from a smaller angle. Estimating that angle was the tricky part. Down on our bellies in the sand, one eye closed, we drew straight lines...one in the direction of the distant tree, one back towards our 90-degree reference point.

Student after student lay down in the sand to redraw those lines and to use his protractor to measure the angle. The measurements varied considerably. How to resolve these discrepancies? Ah-ha! Time to introduce that branch of mathematics known as statistics. We accept *all* the measurements and we take the median! Knowing this angle, and easily measuring the length between the two sighting points on our side of the river, we used our friend from trigonometry, the *tangent function!* Twenty textbooks flew open. Who could find the tangent of 53 degrees? Twenty pencils began calculating. Do we multiply or divide? Several women washing clothes looked up and laughed at us. What the heck were we doing?

OK, we've got the answer. We know the width of the river without having crossed it. That's the point! That's the power of trigonometry! *Professeur,* a student asked, "how do we know our calculation is accurate?" *Bon question!* I replied. We have seen the power of trigonometry, but let us always question our methods and procedures. Let's find out just how accurate our prediction really is. So I send a student wading across the river with a string. The river is no more than a few feet deep, but the current is swift. He holds one end of the string by the tree on the distant bank and we hold the other end. We measure the string and...*Mon Dieu!* Our prediction was amazingly accurate. Just a meter or so off.

Back together on one shore the students are joyfully celebrating. I'm thrilled too, because I can see they have learned something today that could not be taught in a classroom. They're joking around; I'm trying to direct the conversion towards an analysis of the possible sources of our error.

And then it happens. A woman washing clothes lets out a bloodcurdling scream. We look up and see a child lying on the rocks, surrounded by people. The African child is a startling blue color. A man is holding the child, slapping it a bit. Other women wail mournfully. We dash over while a student translates into French for me. The child had been playing while his mother washed clothes. The rocks were slippery, the current was swift. It had taken just a few seconds.

Not breathing, the child appears lifeless. Some people start leaving. I hear murmuring about not wanting to be witnesses for a police investigation. Somewhere in my mind I store the observation that fear of bureaucratic hassles is not just an American condition.

It's obvious that what's needed is mouth-to-mouth resuscitation. I had learned it in a swimming class, or did they teach it in Peace Corps training? Stay cool, I tell myself, and keep your sense of timing. My lips on the child's... exhale only a short breath... remember it's a child... hand on his diaphragm...feel for expansion... good... pace myself... slowly.. .take a breath and try again...slowly...again...slowly...again. The child begins to breathe! Still blue, but breathing.

OK, that's all I know. Let's get the kid to the clinic. He's in my arms. A student says he's just seen the town ambulance nearby, but it was delivering cement. OK, let's walk. The students follow. A truck stops. The driver tells us to get in and takes us to the clinic. There they splash rubbing alcohol on the kid's back. He's fine now, crying fiercely, but fine! Let's go home.

Two days later, a woman shows up at my door. She is wailing and talking too fast in Kabrais. It was hard enough for me to learn French. I never mastered Kabrais. A neighbor translates for me. It is the child's mother. She literally kisses my feet. I am embarrassed. I tell her I am happy that her son was well.

A few people in town thanked me. My students talked about it a bit. Inside I felt great about it. A child lives because of me. Monday morning we're back in class. OK, we've learned about sine and cosine, but what about secant and cosecant? There's more to study, and we've got to prepare for those important national exams coming in June.

Senegal, West Africa

First Day

By Susan Rosenfeld (Senegal 1977-81)

I walked down the road, hoping I would never reach my destination. Please, I thought, half seriously, half jokingly, let me be hit by a car and then I'll never have to face them.

Despite ten weeks of intensive preparation in Senegal and a master's degree with a year's preparation in the States before that, I knew I was not ready.

Finally I reached my destination, unharmed by any vehicle. The destination was College de la Petite Cote, a Catholic secondary school in the coastal fishing town of Joal. They were not enemies, monsters, or ogres, but my students; for it was the first day of school.

The bell rang and my heart sank. There was no putting it off any longer. Why did I ever think I wanted to do this? I wondered. The students lined up and marched into the classroom.

There were forty of them, half boys and half girls. They

sat there quietly and expectantly, waiting to see what their American teacher would be like.

"Good morning, class."

"Good morning, Miss."

"How are you?"

"Fine, Thank you. And you?"

"Fine, thank you."

Well, I thought, this is going very well. Maybe this won't be so bad after all. Their *sixieme* teacher (first year of English) had trained them very well.

I plunged into what I had meticulously been preparing for several days.

"Now, I want everyone (gesture, just the way I was taught—the whole class) to have a notebook and a pen (just as I was trained, waving a notebook and pen around the room) and bring them to class every day."

Blank stares.

Patiently: "Class, a pen (waving my blue Bic) and a notebook (waving my notebook); you bring them every day!"

Blank stares. A few students begin to squirm uncomfortably.

"What's the matter?"

One brave student ventures, "Miss, we don't understand. You don't speak English."

Don't speak English?! I wasn't ready for that one. I had steeled myself for lots of noise, giggles, unruly kids, and spit-balls—but being told, five minutes into the school year, that I didn't speak English, that was unexpected.

"I don't speak English?"

"Non," responded forty kids, brightly and politely.

"What do I speak then?"

"On ne sait pas, Miss, mais ce n'est pas de l'anglais," offered one bold soul, rather apologetically.

Switching into French, which I had promised myself I would never, *never* use, I asked, "What do you mean I don't speak English? I'm from America."

"Yes, Miss, but you don't speak good English like Mr.

Benoit. He spoke good English. We could understand him. Your accent is bad."

"Who is Mr. Benoit?"

"Our English teacher last year."

"Oh, I see. And what nationality is he?"

"He's Senegalese, Miss."

"And what's his native language?"

"Serrere, Miss."

"And where did he learn his English?"

"In school."

"And what nationality am I?"

"American."

"And where did I learn English?"

"At home."

"So, if someone's accent is 'bad,' whose do you think it is?"

Silence, in the face of this irrefutable logic.

"But," I said, brightly, not wanting to put down Mr. Benoit in front of his students, "perhaps neither accent is bad. Perhaps they're just different."

Relief flooded the students' faces. "Yes, Miss," they say, "because Mr. Benoit was a good teacher. A very, very, very good teacher. The best. We hope you'll do things just like him."

I'll have to check this out, I thought. Who is this Benoit character anyhow?

The rest of the hour proceeded uneventfully. A review of the present tense. Personal pronouns. Question words. I was amazed. They're actually accepting me as a teacher! They think it's normal that I stand up here in front of them and gesticulate and call on them and correct them. The other teachers think it's normal that I'm a teacher. The director thinks it's normal. I guess it doesn't show that I don't know what I'm doing. I wonder if this feeling will ever go away...?

The Peace Corps is respected in this country because Volunteers have sacrificed comfort and consumption to do a job in the developing world; because this country respects adventure, voluntary spirit, and the desire to help others.

The Peace Corps is respected abroad because volunteers have often done the different jobs no one else was able or willing to do; because Volunteers have filled needs for trained manpower at critical times. Moreover, the Peace Corps comes without strings or ulterior motive, separate from American foreign policy, with no other purpose than to help where needed.

Joseph H. Blatchford
Peace Corps Director
1969-1971

Morocco, North Africa

Neighbors

by Orin Hargraves (Morocco 1980-82)

It was a hot, dusty afternoon in late August. I had just returned to El Hajeb, the village where I had taught English for a year. I'd been away for the summer: a few weeks of being surrounded by Volunteers old and new at that year's omnibus training program in Rabat, the capital. El Hageb was a big come-down after all that. I was the only American in town, and though I'd been quite happy with that for a year, coming back to it all at once was a shock. I hadn't yet rediscovered any of the parts about it that I liked.

I spent most of the afternoon writing letters, catching up on correspondence that had piled up in my mailbox while I was away. I was also conveniently avoiding the heat, and, to some degree, the village itself. At the moment it didn't feel like the place I wanted to be. I stayed inside the thick, cool, stuccoed walls of my fine house. You see, mine wasn't the mud-hut Peace Corps experience. I lived in the upstairs apartment of a beautiful colonial-period villa in the part of the town that had been built by the French. Walnut trees lined the avenue outside, and I could hear boys throwing stones up into them, trying to knock down the ripening fruit.

A cool breeze from the mountains picked up late in the afternoon, intimating that it might bring some clouds our way, along with a shower or thunderstorm. I took advantage of the cooler air to get a little exercise and walked to the post office. I felt fortified now after the hours of cool seclusion, ready to withstand the stares of the children, and the cries of "Christian! Christian!" that often accompanied me on my walks in the village.

The post office offered the usual experience: a cluster of people mashed together in front of the sullen clerk, all thrusting their business in his face, with a line of the less determined off to one side, standing patiently in the belief that they would be waited on sometime. I joined the line, not yet feeling up to the cluster experience. It took ten minutes or so, but this way I could stay inside the thick American shell that I still wasn't willing to come out of.

When I started back, the rain was looking like a sure thing. The breeze had become a wind. Little dust devils were whirling around in the dirt streets, and withered leaves twirled down from the sycamore trees that formed an arcade over the wide, dilapidated street. Dark clouds were bearing down from the mountains to the south. I picked up my pace, thinking that now I'd have to hurry to get in before the rain.

Down the street, coming towards me, was a woman wrapped up in a turquoise jellaba. I recognized her as my downstairs neighbor. She wasn't veiled and her hood was off: this was only a walk in the neighborhood and she wouldn't be subject to the prying eyes of students. As we continued toward each other, we were nearly jogging, trying to reach our destinations before the rain. Under these circumstances, the normal greeting rituals—which could run to a few minutes of chattering even with someone that you saw all the time— would be overlooked. We only exchanged the minimum smiles and hello, how-are-yous as we passed.

"Please tell Aisha to put the goats in the shed, it's going to rain," she shouted at me over her shoulder as she continued on her way.

"OK," I said.

In that moment, such a feeling of elation! And why, over something so small and trivial? Because she said it in Arabic, not in French. Because she didn't slow down or dress it up for speaking to a foreigner. Because she said it to me in the same way she would have said it to one of her own children, or one of her other neighbors: without formality, without any awareness that she was talking to someone from the other side of the world, but just saying it the way she would normally say it. Because after all I was only her neighbor, no one strange or special. I was just the guy who lived upstairs.

The significance of the description, Returned Peace Corps Volunteer, is becoming more and more apparent as the thousands of RPCV's continue to give of themselves back home in the United States. Peace Corps Volunteers upon completion of service aren't called "ex-volunteers" or "former volunteers." The Third Goal of the Peace Corps Act spelled out that the PCV's were responsible to share their newly acquired knowledge of their host country with the people of America. Therefore, the description "Returned" was applied to show that these individuals were still associated with the Peace Corps and more particularly with the Act that enabled them to serve overseas.

Information gathered by the National Peace Corps Association attests to the variety of Volunteer activities RPCVs perform that go far beyond the vision of the Third Goal. And all of these activities continue the Peace Corps spirit of giving one one's self to assist others.

Kevin O'Donnell
Peace Corps Director
1971-1972

Seychelles, Indian Ocean

Going Home By Tata

by Charles Kastner (Seychelles 1980-81)

In the early evening, tired workers began arriving at the main bus stop, a flat area of dry red dirt, dotted with sheds. They carried large cloth handbags filled with tools, or food bought from the central market: pork or fish wrapped in brown paper, bananas, jack fruit, or papaya.

The workers joined me on the flat wooden benches, sheltered by a corrugated tin roof. We were waiting for the Beau Vallon to take us away from Victoria, the capital city and principal port of the Seychelles, an equatorial nation of a hundred-odd islands sprinkled in the middle of the Indian Ocean. The bus traveled over the high granite spine of Mahe, the largest island in the Seychelles, and down to the tourist hotels on Beau Vallon Beach. Most of the passengers lived in the highlands above the city, at St. Louis Bel Air or Pascal Village, where the air is cooler and the smell of the city is replaced by the scent of flowers, cooking food, and mist.

I was the only non-Seychellois at the stop—most of the

tourists avoid the buses around 4 o'clock—but I did not feel out of place. I felt like a local and chattered away with the man about the everyday things of life: his children, the heat, the price of fish at the local market.

The bus arrived and everyone headed toward the open door of the Tata, the local name for the big green and white buses that provide public transportation on the island. I'd fumbled with my bag and was a step or two behind most of the people. I found myself on the periphery, edged out by more stoutly built or more agile individuals. The bus filled up fast as more and more Seychellois pushed through the door into the shadowy interior of the bus. As the mass compressed to ten or so individuals my chance came. I managed to grip the railing and squeeze myself up the stairs. People crowded the stairwell behind me, but the bus driver waved them off.

The lucky passengers sat in the worn green seats and adjusted themselves and their belongings for the ride. The rest of us stood patiently with our bags stuck between our feet and one hand gripping the steel railing that ran the length of the roof. We were glad to be here, freed from the hassle of waiting for the next bus or looking for alternative transportation. No one spoke much, content it seemed to quietly review the events of the day or prepare for the routines of evening.

My day had been good, another one to add to my list of Peace Corps memories and minor triumphs. I taught physical education to physically and mentally challenged children, and that afternoon, several of the Seychellois teachers and I had decided to take our blind students running. We loaded the kids into the school van and took them to a secluded beach that curved in a graceful inward arc for about a mile. The sand was hard-packed beneath my feet. The beach, like most everything on Mahe, was vividly beautiful, with the brilliant blues of the tropical ocean, glittering white sand, and the bright greens of the foliage framed by the rough, eroded granite cliffs.

When we assembled at this idyllic spot, I placed a sighted teacher with two blind students. The teacher had the job of running between the two and giving them verbal cues to keep them headed in the right direction. Most of the kids managed to run the length of the beach, a major feat for children who had never run for more than a few hundred yards. The best moment of the day came when a student told me that the run had set him free for the first time in his life. I was happy that I'd had a hand in planting that idea. It was another small accomplishment that I filed away in my memory.

The start of the bus engine brought me back to the present. I breathed in the diesel fumes mixed with the scent of packed bodies, fresh fish, raw meat, and ripe fruit in the equatorial heat. My nose tingled as the bus entered the main road. I stood directly behind the bus driver, looking out the front window as we climbed away from Victoria. I gripped the hand hold and watched the driver navigate the bus up the winding mountain road. I gripped the rail even harder when a descending Tata met us on a hairpin corner. Both drivers jammed on their brakes and the two giants moved gingerly past each other on the narrow road, their side mirrors nearly colliding. Our driver, long accustomed to these encounters, was unfazed by the incident and casually smiled and waved at his fellow Tata driver. I regripped the steel bar, calmed my pounding heart, and pressed my bag tightly between my legs.

My legs relaxed when we reached the top of the hill and my stop at St. Louis Bel Air. The bus pulled off the road and about ten of us got off. I chatted with some of them as I made the slow walk up the patched side road to my neighborhood, a quiet place on the border of Morne Seychellois National Park. The small stucco houses of the neighborhood hugged the granite side of the mountain and held back the jungle of the park. I loved the place. It stood above the heat of the city and filled my mind with memories—fruit bats floating on the quiet air currents of moonlit nights, cool mist hugging the mountaintops in early morning, and the fragrance of flowers from our garden perfuming the air.

I lived with Mary, my wife and fellow Peace Corps Volunteer, in the first house on the right side of the road, a small house with a red tiled roof, wide windows and doors, and a beautiful flower garden. The left side was too steep to build on. Between our house and the next was a foot path that led up to a small farm where a kindly old man and woman raised pigs and chickens. Every night "Madam" came home balancing a huge bundle of greenery on her head for their pigs. The third house up the street belonged to Jeff and Ruth, good friends who taught us how to cook Seychellois foods and who laughed at our accents and our imperfect Creole.

The open door to my house told me that Mary had beaten me home from her job as nutritionist at Victoria Hospital. Jeff waved to me from his yard and came over to talk. I had made it home.

Jamaica, West Indies

That Rascal, Melvin

by Camilla Griffiths (Jamaica 1985-87)

As I turned the corner into the green, grassy courtyard of the hospital, I saw a small barefoot boy in typical, white ill-fitting hospital shorts and slipover. A handsome boy, about four feet tall with fine features and smooth, closely cut hair, he strutted along with shoulders back. He sang in a strong, screechy voice: "Jesus pon de telefone. Tel him what ya need, tel him wat ya need rite now. I don wan silva. I don wan gol. I just wan Jesus inna me sol."

From that moment, getting to know Melvin Diah was an up-and-down experience. As a Peace Corps Volunteer, I was assigned to be a teacher/play leader in this pediatric ward of the University Hospital of the West Indies in Kingston, Jamaica. My function was to help lonely, frightened, and bored children adapt to the hospital scene and, I hoped, to stimulate an interest in learning.

On my first day, Melvin jerked away from me as I tried to get him back to the room he shared with six other children. He grabbed my hand and bit the back of it before giving in. The next morning I was concerned about another attack as he ran up to me. But in an excited voice he called out "Teacha, Teacha!" He reached for that same hand and kissed it. I was puzzled and intrigued.

I came under the spell of this five-year-old during my two years there. He was a long-term patient whose parents visited infrequently. They could not afford the bus fare or the time from their endless search for income. Melvin's place of residence was listed as "Railway Premises," some fifteen miles away from Spanish Town. This simply meant he lived in a thrown-up shack in the railway yard. Adequate post-hospitalization care was not possible there. Having mistaken cleaning fluid for a fruit drink at the age of three, Melvin had a severely burned esophagus. The medical treatment was successful, but he had to remain in the hospital, since his eating had to be carefully monitored. Because he was not bedridden, this super-charged young dynamo was on the loose much of the day.

One day a small frightened child was wheeled to the operating *teata* accompanied by a student nurse, no family member present. I heard Melvin call out to him, "Take care, ya hear?" He was in charge. He tried to control the nurses—yes, me also!

This very young boy was an incredible composite: sharp, fearless, shameless, loveable, dishonest, sensitive, irresponsible, charming, disarming, crafty, and amusing. I could see it all in his sparkling eyes.

Working with children of mixed ages, I tried to strengthen an understanding of the alphabet, reading and writing. Melvin was a quick learner—if I could get him to sit still long enough. My school supplies were limited, but he always tried to walk from the classroom with a fistful of used computer paper, even though my limit was two sheets per child. Deftly folding the paper into the shape of a handgun, he made several for his compatriots. Acutely aware of the prevalence of street crime in Jamaican society, I said, "Melvin,

I hate guns! I will *not* have guns in my classroom!" "Yes, Teacha" was the reply from this face that was suddenly all innocence. But under his mattress was an arsenal of paper weapons to supply all the gunmen out there.

One day a Jamaican clergyman, eyes closed, clutching his Bible to his chest and placing his hand on Melvin's head, prayed for health. Melvin wore his solemn mask—until he caught sight of me, then his mischievous twinkle returned.

Finally, he was able to go home. About to depart after a nine-month stay, he stood encircled by the doctor and nursing staff as they counseled him to go to school and be very careful about what entered his mouth. His upturned serious face expressed a commitment to living according to their rules. With a hug and a wave, I said "Take care, ya hear." He left an empty spot on the ward—and in my heart.

A few months later, as I brought a toy to a child in the overcrowded ward, I heard that familiar voice call out raspingly and tearfully, "Teacha." I could not believe it! Melvin was back and he was hurting. He had been eating a genip, a small green sweet fruit with a very large smooth and slippery pit, which he swallowed, tearing his fragile esophagus. He was taken to the *teata,* where careful surgery repaired the damage.

When he was returned to the ward, subdued as I had never expected to see him, I stood over his bed, which was protected by scarred guard rails. "How many sheets of paper do you want, Melvin?" Although he was not completely free of the control of the anesthetic, he slowly held up five fingers. Melvin was back.

Going on with my life in the States I think of that rascal, Melvin, a teenager by now. If I had the chance to see him again I would grab it, but how would I find him? Does he still reside at the Railway Premises? What kind of mischief might he be into now?

Volunteers I have known left varied but positive and indelible influences overseas, whether on the job to which they were assigned, in the community where they lived, or with the many people of the country who came to know them and their contributions. In turn, the Volunteers gained insight not only to themselves but especially an appreciation and respect for differences... of cultures, values, and philosophies.

Donald. K. Hess
Peace Corps Director
1972-1973

Lesotho, Southern Africa

In a Pig's Eye

by Matt Losak (Lesotho 1985-88)

I could hear the boys in their rising clamor of bloodlust. They were preparing to slaughter the pigs, a ritual that I had come to dread. After eighteen months, I knew what to expect.

Frustrated by the noise of the slaughter, I tried to drown it out with the Irish mood music of Enya. My mother had sent the tape with a letter describing the wedding and a funeral I had missed, and the porch screen that needed my attention. Looking up from the letter, I stared across the soccer field at the women and their cookpots, which stood near the cafeteria of the Catholic mission school where I taught. My village was on a plateau surrounded by a formidable circle of jagged mountaintops. At the edge of the plateau, beyond the school, were the animals—the pig sties, the chicken coops, the over-milked cow and the tired oxen. They eyed the approaching boys with stoic suspicion.

I did not object to killing pigs for food. I had accepted

the realities and indignities of farm life—the stench of the outhouse, the gore and fuss of butchering chickens—long before my arrival from New York City. However, I had come to rest my sanity on the belief that the universal behavior of human beings would always produce basically the same feelings and reactions to the world that I had. In my village, I knew smart people and dullards, comedians and Casanovas. They were all there, just as they had been in New York City.

Only occasionally did a moment or an event shake this belief and make me mutter to myself little arguments that something was tolerable or acceptable or unavoidable when my heart and head told me that it wasn't. The sadism of these boys—bright, sensitive boys who were learning Shakespeare this week—disturbed me. I went through the same old arguments: "This is their country...in their culture they believe...it's not my place...they don't understand and if I try to explain it to them...I can't change the world..." and so on. The week before, I had confidently told a group of new Peace Corps arrivals how to live in southern Africa. The boys were reminding me how little I really knew.

I sat down with a novel and was momentarily comfortable until an unusually high scream from one of the torture victims rang out. I decided that I couldn't take it any longer. Africa or no, Peace Corps Volunteer or no, I was not going to sit idly by as my students caused innocent animals needless pain.

I would go to Nils for help, I thought. Nils was my neighbor, a member of the Danish Volunteer Service, who had an expert knowledge of pigs from a decade or so of pig farming in Denmark. In addition to his expertise, Nils was nearly seven feet tall and towered over my small, skinny students. If he couldn't change their thinking, perhaps Nils could at least intimidate the boys into containing their glee and showing some respect to the animals.

But Nils was no help.

"Go get a ball-peen hammer from the wood shop, hold the pig by the ears and give it a wallop between the eyes.

Don't worry about the squealing," Nils said. "Pigs squeal the same whether you pet them or cut them. The hammer will knock it flat out. Then you can cut its throat with the heart still beating, and bleed it painlessly to death," he said in a matter-of-fact voice, as if describing how to build a model airplane.

Nils never slaughtered animals, I learned, and didn't like to be around when they were killed. Even after ten years of pig farming, he explained, he always packed his animals off to be "dressed."

A sustained squeal followed by the thudding sound of an animal being kicked spun me on my heel toward the boys. Not on my watch, I thought. There were some things I could be culturally sensitive about because these people had a different "style" of humanity, but I knew that even the mothers and fathers of these kids would not permit them to be needlessly cruel.

This was a boarding school for the best and the brightest from villages around the country. Wasn't it my responsibility as a teacher to impose some moral guidance, to offer a more decent approach to living? I charged across the soccer field, my head held high. A familiar feeling of confidence rose in me. It was the way I used to feel when I rushed from the locker room to the playing field with a herd of football players.

There were about fifteen boys who had formed a circle around three pigs. Also present was the school principal, Modeekee, who seemed to be enjoying the sport as much as anybody. What an example, I thought to myself. I shouted at all of them, "I think that's enough!" trying hard not to lose my composure. The voices of reason were again rising in my head: Try to see it their way...Don't be too self-righteous...Be respectful of other customs... and so on.

I failed in my attempt to be calm. "Why are you torturing these animals? Why don't you respect them? They are giving their lives for you to eat their meat!" I declared, sounding like a wild-eyed prophet admonishing the sinners.

"Yes. It is true," said Modeekee, trying to placate me.

Nathaniel, one of my best students, attempted to explain in a way that I would find convincing. "It is their time, sir. They have lived a lazy life doing nothing for their food and now they must pay the price." He smiled at his own cleverness. The others nodded approvingly.

As a teacher, even a new one, I had learned a few things about my students. They only respected my authority if I could turn an argument back on the arguer. Having failed countless times already, I had a few ready replies. "May we then torture the students for not doing their homework?" Not great, I thought, but not bad for the spur of the moment.

"No, sir!" they shouted together. Modeekee smiled politely. Feeling that I had won the moment with my righteousness and wit, I took the opportunity to suggest my alternative. I shouted orders. I needed a ball-peen hammer from the wood shop, and a sharp knife. "Stand by with the kerosene." The boys were disappointed that they were not allowed to light the pigs while they were still alive, scraping off the first layer of trembling, hairy skin with the tips of their shovels. No. We were ready to begin a new way of doing things, more humane, more efficient, more skillful.

Excited that I was going to show them a new technology from the United States, the boys and the vice-principal tightened the circle around me and the largest of the three pigs. As word spread of the unfolding spectacle, other students added themselves to the ranks. Near the edge of the crowd the two remaining pigs were tied to stakes, condemned to watch the slaughter that foretold their own. Holding the shiny hammer high, I rotated it so that it caught the afternoon sun and captured the group's attention. I was going to hold the pig by the ear, I said, and whack it between the ears, presumably crushing its frontal lobe. Then, while its heart still beat, I would cut its throat and empty the blood into the bowl that the students kept on hand so that they could drink the blood—no waste here.

Modeekee interrupted to make a suggestion. "Perhaps if

you just hold him on his side and put your knife in here," he said, pointing to the spot in the rib cage just over the heart, "you will kill him very painlessly and quickly."

The pig looked at me. I had to answer politely. Modeekee's proposal was an accepted method, done without the torturous fanfare, but I had seen too many pigs bawl minute after minute, their blood a fountain. I also had seen the knifeman miss, then dig frantically for the central organ. I listened to Modeekee, appearing to consider his point of view carefully, then explained that this new method would be at least as effective, and less noisy.

I knew that I had begun to fall back on wishful thinking, and so did Modeekee. He was in his forties, and taller and bigger than any of us. While his unusual stature had more to do with his authority than his intellect did, his years had at least educated him in the ways of know-it-all young men. To his credit, he was offering me a way out with fatherly tact. Too late for that; I was now set on doing the right thing my way.

Holding the swine by the ear and raising the heavy hammer over my head, I squatted down and drew the circle of eyes to the shiny weapon, repeating my mantra about the importance of a painless death for the animals we eat. I directed two of the younger boys to sharpen their knives and to be ready. The group seemed to fold its arms as one. The pig, grunting and leaning away from me, gave a look of supplication as I brought the hammer down.

I knew before the hammer struck that it was all wrong. The weight of the instrument grew heavier as I held it up for my brief lecture. The pig seemed to figure out my strategy, and in one blunderous smash my hammer met the pig's suddenly upturned snout with a crunching thud, knocking most of the pig's mouth down its throat.

Its screams echoed crazily in its pain. I clung to its ear as we spun, screwing ourselves deeper and deeper into the mud. I brought the hammer down again and again, its weight growing so heavy that I could no longer hold it properly. The flat of the hammer fell dully on the animal. The crowd roared.

Finally, in sudden silence, I sat in the mud holding the twisted ear of the barely conscious beast. I dropped the hammer and ordered the two boys holding their knives to cut the pig's throat. They hesitated, as people do when shock and spectacle collide. Another order got no response as I slowly pulled myself to my feet. Modeekee was looking grave and a trifle smug. He nodded at the boys, who sprang into action.

"Well, that's it," I said, handing the hammer to my smartest, who looked at me with an ironic, you've-got-to-be-kidding expression. "Don't miss, and you're all set," I said, clapping the dirt from my hands and the seat of my pants, as if all had gone as planned.

My head felt light and my body heavy as I carried myself away. My feet rose and fell as if my shoes were made of lead. My arms swung straight and dejected from their sockets. As I neared my house, I could hear laughter behind me, followed by a hush.

Then came the screaming of the last two pigs.

Cameroon, West Africa

Death and Life in the Peace Corps

By Jacqueline Gold (Cameroon 1987-89)

I n the early hours of the morning, when my brain has just started the slow swim towards consciousness, the cries of children and the sounds of cars rattling below my window are deceptive. These are the universal noises of an awakening day, and in my semi-slumber I can believe that I'm abed in a split-level ranch house on a tree-lined street of North America, not under an army-issue mosquito net in a mud-brick, tin-roofed town in Africa.

Then the goat bleats. Loudly. And I am awake and fully aware than this is Cameroon and I am in the Peace Corps. My eyes fall on the bamboo wardrobe that holds my T-shirts and cotton drawstring pants. A huge burnt-sienna cockroach scuttles across the floor.

The goat, tied by a piece of thin black rubber to a garbage pile next to my house, bleats again. He is the only organized system of waste disposal in the compound where I live, and his raucous morning speech serves to get me out of bed.

A key turns in the lock of my front door and Helen, the woman who does my laundry and keeps the house dust at bay, enters. *"Nshaela,"* I call out, good morning. *"Alecho?"* How are you? She repeats the greetings, but having almost exhausted my knowledge of the Dschang dialect, we quickly switch to French.

She is only here to bring me bread, she tells me, placing a long crusty baguette on the dining room table. Her *petite souer* (little sister) has died in childbirth, hemorrhaging in her own blood, and Helen must now tramp the ten kilometers to her village to attend the *doy*. We debate the possible causes of the woman's death.

Helen is not as grief-stricken as one might expect, partially because family tragedy is so common here, but also because *petite souer* is a misnomer. The woman is really not related to Helen at all, but comes from her village, the second largest in Cameroon. It is possible that had they run into each other on the street they would not have known each another.

Still, a death in the village is a big event and I know Helen shouldn't miss the wake.

I get dressed cursing the filth and carelessness of the Dschang Hospital, which Helen's *petite souer* walked halfway across the town to get to, only to die in delivery. Helen says the woman had been to see a local *guerrisseur*, a traditional doctor, who prescribed killing a young chicken and spilling its blood on the floor of her house to ensure a safe birth. Helen had heard that when the woman brought the chicken home and was sharpening a knife to cut its throat, the fowl mysteriously disappeared. Helen insists the woman's failure to let the chicken's blood run caused the hemorrhaging.

Depressed by the news and by a world view that blames a death on an escaped chicken, I set off for work. I walk past the bush-taxi park where creaking vans loaded with people, pigs, goats, chickens, cocoa yams and plantains provide public transport.

The community development office where I work is

empty, save for building technician Samuel Tatah Ngeh, and Justine Kenfack, our typist, who is asleep at her desk, her head lying on folded arms. Justine is pregnant with her fifth child, which may explain why she is always so tired.

"Hello," Sam says, and slaps my hand in a shake that ends with the snapping of our fingers, one against the other. "Look what has come for you." He points to a crumpled plastic bag filled with 1000-franc bills. "The head of the village development committee has returned the 50,000 francs. You have done well. That discussion with the Canadian Embassy succeeded. You are a very powerful woman."

I look in the bag incredulously. Canadian Embassy foreign aid slated for a village health center had mysteriously been transferred from the project account to the personal bank account of the man who heads the village development committee. I had come across this transaction only by accident, when the committee head failed to provide the necessary receipts to justify project expenses. After many unanswered letters to the man demanding an explanation, I chased him down in the capital of a neighboring province. The confrontation seems to have scared him into returning the money.

"I've heard that this man is applying to other embassies to get more aid for his village," I tell Sam. "Perhaps he didn't want a poor write-up from the Canadians to ruin his chances with the Dutch or the British." I am relieved to get the money back. We have already had one contractor run off without building what he was paid to build, and the electric generator that cost more than a million francs to purchase from Japan via Nigeria is already two months late in arriving.

Sam and I borrow an old British Land Rover from the agriculture office and battle the road dust for a butt-slamming hour up into the mountains to the village where the health center is under construction. Near the village, the leaves of the banana trees are still damp and green, not covered in the rustoleum of red dust as the foliage is closer to town. The coffee is in bloom and the unpaved road quickly turns to troughs of mud.

The newly painted health center looks like a turquoise green palace set in the midst of the jungle. Sam and I tour the building with a government health worker, a tall, mustachioed anglophone man in a white lab jacket. He and Sam talk rapidly in pidgin, brother anglophones in this francophone bush.

I wander into a dark room with several misshapen wrought iron beds. In one corner is a baby's trundle bed and three women lying or sitting on the beds to either side of it.

"Metsadi," I greet them in Dschang. They laugh and cover their faces with their hands. A white woman speaking Dschang! What excitement!

An older woman in mourning black, a black kerchief covering her head, grabs my hand and begins rattling away in dialect, gesturing toward the baby and alternately at one of the young women.

"Il y a quelqu'un qui peut parlet francais?" I ask hopefully.

Yes, one of the younger women speaks French. She gave birth Saturday night. She introduces the new baby girl and the woman in black, her mother.

I turn toward the trundle bed where a fat cocoa-colored baby gurgles happily. She wears a pink crocheted bonnet and matching button-down sweater. I touch the baby's cheek and admire the knitting.

Congratulations, I say. She is beautiful. Did you make this pullover?

Yes, the young woman grins proudly.

It is very nicely made, I tell her.

Sam and the health worker have come up behind me and are watching over my shoulder as the baby pulls at her bonnet strings.

I introduce Sam to the woman. He looks embarrassed, but greets the woman in French.

The health worker in the lab jacket points to me and tells the woman that I am responsible for getting the health center finished, which sends them into a flurry of handshakes and *"Merci, Madame."* It is a slight exaggeration of my role as project administrator, but I blush and feel proud.

I turn to him and congratulate him for delivering the healthy baby. "I heard only this morning of a woman who died giving birth at the Dschang Hospital last night. And you, you have done this out here in the middle of nowhere. You have a lot to be proud of."

He looks happily embarrassed.

The three of us start to leave the room and I call out *"Mbo, ee-ee,"* so long, bye-bye to the women. This sets off a gale of giggles, hands slapping across faces to hide their glee.

Sam and I climb into the Land Rover for the roller-coaster ride back to town. It's been another day of death and life.

What has always struck me most about Peace Corps Volunteers, regardless of their background or skill, is the depth of their caring "gene." If they have an abundance of that trait, they are more likely to have a successful Peace Corps experience and, for that matter, life.

Nicholas W. Craw
Peace Corps Director
1973-1974

Rwanda, Central Africa

Kunga (or ... No Hard Feelings)

by Andrew L. Thomas (Rwanda 1988-90)

My house in the village of Kirambo, Rwanda was six kilometers from the spectacular mountaintop research station where I worked as a Peace Corps Volunteer, conducting agricultural research and doing extension work. I rode my Honda-185 motorcycle up and down the mountain nearly every day to the station, and also back and forth at lunchtime, so nearly everyone along the way knew me. The narrow dirt road passed through a small densely populated village called Cyapa at the top of the mountain where many of the station workers lived. People were always walking in the road in Cyapa, and I usually beeped my horn as I slowly passed through the village.

One day I was riding home from work after a long day in the fields, and was traveling through Cyapa as usual. My horn was full of dust and not working, and a loud gasoline-powered flour mill was also making a lot of noise, so a drunk man stumbling down the road did not hear me approaching. I slowed way down as I tried to maneuver around him, but as I neared and he finally heard me approaching, he was startled and unexpectedly ran right in front of me. I was barely moving at that point and didn't hit him, but somehow, while I was dumping the motorcycle in trying to avoid him, he ended up on the ground with the front wheel on top of him. He was not hurt at all; he was just startled and maybe humiliated and a little dusty.

A crowd quickly gathered and even though the man was obviously not hurt, they insisted that I carry him on my motorcycle to the nearby clinic, which I did. I knew the local "doctor" would prescribe a "pomade" (a Ben-gay type of skin ointment), as he did for everything, so I told the man I would pay for the pomade if he brought me the receipt.

I heard nothing more about the incident for several weeks. But one day I got a memo from the Rwandan station director saying that the man, Mr. Bizimana, wanted some sort of compensation from me for the incident. Soon after that, Mr. Bizimana appeared at my office. When I asked him for the receipt for the pomade, he didn't have one, because of course he had never bought (or needed) it. He proceeded hesitantly to explain to me that he wanted 200 francs (about $2.00) to settle for his pain and suffering!

I was furious because of course Mr. Bisimana had not been hurt, and it was partially his fault anyway for running in front of the motorcycle. But the station director suggested I just go ahead and pay the "fine" to make sure everything about the incident was settled. He suggested I go to the parquet (local court) in Kirambo, discuss it with the judge, and have Mr. Bizimana sign something to be certain that nothing more would come of the affair. I went and talked to the judge and he concurred that this was a fairly normal way of settling such incidents in Rwanda.

My neighbor and best friend, Aaron, happened to work at the parquet and agreed to type up an "official" release for each of us to sign. All concerned were to meet the following day at noon at the parquet to sign the paper as I turned over the 200 francs.

The next day, I rode to the parquet at noon and everything proceeded as arranged. Mr. Bizimana and I, along with the several witnesses, signed the paper, and I gave the man the money. I was still rather angry and disgusted by the whole affair, and soon put on my motorcycle helmet in preparation to go home. As I prepared to start the motorcycle, everyone looked at me, startled and disbelieving. They asked where I was going. I explained that I was not all that pleased by the situation and just wanted to be done with it, go home, and eat lunch.

Aaron, also quite perplexed about my wanting to leave, then carefully explained to me that since Mr. Bizimana had just collected 200 francs, he and I, Aaron, the judge, and all the witnesses were going to the bar, and Mr. Bizimana was buying beer for everyone with his newly-acquired riches! Aaron insisted that I come, as this was the normal and proper thing to do. I could tell that Mr. Bizimana really did not want to do this either. He would have preferred just to leave with the money, but he obviously knew he had no choice in the matter.

So the whole group went together to the bar. Aaron made sure I sat next to Mr. Bizimana as he ordered bottles of Primus beer and plenty of local banana beer for everyone. As the beers were poured, we all became quite lighthearted, and, after a while, Mr. Bizimana and I were chatting away. After he had spent most of his 200 francs on beer, the judge, Aaron, and I all bought even more beer and we all had a great time. As we finally left the bar in jovial spirits a couple of hours later, Mr. Bizimana and I shook hands, parting as friends, and I really felt that any hostility between us had been put to rest.

This method of settling ill feelings in small communities is a well-established and successful custom in Rwanda. There is even a word for it: *Kunga*. Perhaps we should consider giving Kunga a try in the U.S., but such a wonderful custom would undoubtedly only be possible in the so-called "Third World."

At the heart of effective service in Peace Corps is a meaningful concern for others. Aimed at Peace Corps' basic goal of promoting world peace and friendship, it ends in a win/win/win situation. America gains, the country of service and the world gain, and the committed Volunteer or staffer comes out a big winner.

John R. Dellenback
Peace Corps Director
1975-1977

Liberia, West Africa

Who Will Mind the Garden?

by Paul Eagle (Liberia 1988-90)

I was in Liberia, West Africa, and had been for forty-eight hours. As part of our cross-cultural training, we were each assigned a village and told to stay there for three days, then make our own way home. When we got back, we would discuss our visits, and decide what we needed to work on to make good Peace Corps Volunteers.

Dada Town was my destination, and as I walked down the road I began to wonder if I was heading in the right direction. I passed a group of small mud-brick houses, with tin roofs, the smell of burning wood everywhere. I asked a boy, how far to Dada Town. He turned and ran from me. Faces appeared from nowhere, peering from their doorways. They stared, curious and quiet, as the rain pounded on their roofs and splashed into the puddles. I tried to wipe the rain off my face, but had nothing dry to do it with. I raised my voice to anyone who might answer me. "Dada Town, how far?" An old man pointed ahead and whispered, "Small-far." I looked ahead at the endless greenery divided only by a narrow strip of mud, serving as a road.

We were told in training to eat only food that had been heated and was still warm and that the drinking water they would offer would give us diarrhea or "running belly." So we carried our own. Our trainers taught us the formal "Vai" greeting, which was a beautiful, aggressive, French- sounding dialect, and it was recommended that we use it as much as possible.

Dada Town was smaller than I had expected, forty small houses nestled into a small clearing among the thick trees. The town had one water pump, and perhaps two hundred people. I was immediately greeted and brought into what looked like a central town hall made of mud, stick and corrugated tin. As a crowd gathered inside to stare, a man approached me and shook my hand. He barked, *Ya kunai.* He squeezed firmly, then somehow snapped his middle finger against mine at the same time. We tried it three times and I could not do it. I whispered, *Ya kunai.* His face broke into a wide grin. *Eek boa,* he said. Chuckles and giggles erupted from the sea of dark, curious faces.

An old woman, wearing a colorful *lapa* skirt and a Michigan State tee-shirt, set a bowl of white rice with red oil poured on top, and a huge spoon sticking out of the center, in front of me. I took a few bites, and again Dada Town erupted with laughter, their eyes on my every move. "How da day ma mon?" said one of the men. "It's fine," I said. "But the rain, it can embarrass you?" he quipped. "Yes," I said. Then we sat in silence for almost an hour as the rain pounded the old tin roof. For the first time in forty-eight hours, I started to panic.

Two small boys picked up my backpack and water and led me to a small mud house where I changed into my other pair of wet clothes. An old woman poked her head in the doorway and said, "Brin me do clo." The boy pulled on my muddy tee-shirt, and said, "She will wash your clothes." I peeled it off and handed it to her as she laughed at my bright

The Peace Corps Story

white skin (I did not think about it at the time, but later, I would regret this decision. My clothes were left to dry inside, because of the rain, and did not dry for the duration of my visit.) While I sat in my room, children began streaming in. All of them had protruding bellies, and many had sores on their arms and legs. They were no longer intimidated and began touching my arms. They rubbed my skin and ran their fingers through my hair.

Another woman brought me a bowl of rice. It was the last thing I wanted at the moment, but they all stood and watched until I took a bite. I began to feel like I was on stage. It was unnerving at first, but I began to get used to it. That day, in the rain, I chopped wood, peeled cassava, ground rice, ate tangerines, and walked farms. In each of the tasks, I was outdone by small children, who swung their machetes and used large knives like pros. I had never seen a six-year-old wield a machete, and it was graceful and frightening. After all this activity, I looked down at my watch and saw that it was only 2:00 in the afternoon. Only three hours had passed since I arrived. It was the last time I would look at my watch for three days. I buried it in my backpack.

In the evening, a woman brought me a bucket of hot water. I was puzzled until she made a splashing/washing motion with her hands and I understood that it must be bath time. I had no clue as to how to take a bucket bath. What was the etiquette? Where do I go? What do I use to dry off? A small boy led me to an area with a short bamboo fence surrounding a mound of small rocks. I stood naked, with the rocks poking at my feet, feebly rubbing water all over my body. I dried off with my wet clothes and walked back to my room.

As I lay in bed that night, I felt very alone. At first, I felt terrified and out of control. My fate was completely in the hands of these people. But they had taken perfect care of me so far. As I thought about spending two years in another culture, I began to relax. For the first time in my life, I could truly let go of my inhibitions and open myself up to new experiences. I could not fear what fate would bring, because I did not know what to expect. In fact, I had no idea of what to be afraid of. It was a truly liberating feeling.

It rained all night, and was pouring when I awoke. A woman brought me fried plantain and hot tea, which I ate and drank immediately. I put on my wet clothes and walked out into the muck. School was canceled for the day because of the intense rains, but I wanted to see it anyway, so I walked with a group of children to the schoolhouse.

One section of the mud road was covered with two feet of water where a creek had overflowed. The children laughed as I walked through the water up to my knees. The schoolhouse was built with mud and sticks. A makeshift blackboard leaned against the front wall, with wood benches facing the front of the room. Ten or twelve children had followed me to the school and began holding a "class session."

They wrote their ABC's and words like "cat" and "dog" on the chalkboard. I still could not understand what they were saying, but they pointed and laughed, and I got the general idea of what was going on. Then they sang. They stood in front of me, with their torn shorts, big bellies, bloated from lack of protein, and huge grins, and began to sing in perfect English, with sweet, calm, strong, voices: *Jesus loves the little children/all the children of the world/red and yellow black and white....*

My knees felt wobbly and salt water stung my eyes. As I started sniffling I felt a chill and an unfamiliar lump in my throat getting bigger and bigger. I had been in Africa three days and was sitting in this broken-down schoolhouse with these beautiful Liberian children in front of me as they sang a song of unconditional love. At that moment, I knew I would never be the same.

Almost two years later, I sat in my palaver hut, eating a bowl of rice and red oil with my girlfriend, dog, and a group of children. The fishponds I was working on were coming along well, I had just received a $5,000 grant to build a hospital, and my rural radio show was being broadcast three times a week, translated into six different languages. The evening was cooling off and I was sipping sweet palm wine, brought to me by an old man, who sat in front of me telling stories. While I had been sick with malaria a few times, I had stayed relatively healthy. Paywon and Yogbo, two young boys who had become family to me, ran to bring my guitar and drum and we started playing. We played until the dusk melted into darkness and their mother called them to bed.

The next morning, the BBC reported that rebels had invaded the country. Later, I heard the crunching and spinning of tires coming up our steep hill. A bright blue pickup with the Peace Corps insignia pulled up to the house. "Hello Paul!" chirped the driver as he handed me a letter. Then he sighed, "I'm sorry but you've got an hour to pack. We need to get going. And bring something warm because we don't know where you're headed yet."

While I picked through my accumulated belongings, my neighbors, with whom I had spent the last two years, watched, looking confused. These were people with whom I had shared family problems, pregnancies, births, weddings, holidays, good and bad rice harvests, dances, soccer games, feasts, school meetings, and fishing trips. "It would be better if you don't give your friends any details about your leaving," said the driver, "We wouldn't want to panic anyone." As I was loading my bags into the back of the truck, Paywon, the small boy who helped take care of our garden said, "Mr. Paul, who will mind the garden?" I shook his tiny hand with a snap and didn't cry until I shut the door of the car.

On the highway, makeshift checkpoints had been installed every few miles. An old yellow rope stretched across the road, tied to two garbage cans on either end, held back a long line of cars. Soldiers, their eyes bloodshot and breath smelling of cane juice, slurred questions at us over and over, asking for cigarettes and money.

When we finally made it to the capital, I watched huge trucks filled with young Liberian boys, army recruits, their heads shaved, being hauled 'up country' to fight the rebels. Soldiers were everywhere, and every time a gunshot went off, people fled. Our group waited at the training house for instructions on how and when we were leaving. Liberians began leaving the country in dusty droves. They packed all their belongings into giant "Mandingo" trucks and left their homes for the neighboring countries of Sierra Leone, Guinea, and Ivory Coast. I sat numb, mostly drinking beer and playing cards, trying to decide if I should try to sneak 'up country' and say good-bye to the people who had taken care of me for two years. I couldn't, and it ate away at me as I sat restless and frustrated on an old, torn couch in the burning heat.

Hours later—with no training, no preparation—Peace Corps Volunteers were thrust back into American life. We stood in lines under glaring spotlights, as impersonal U.S. Embassy staff checked our baggage and handed us our tickets. I remember feeling like I was suddenly on the fast-forward mode of a videotape player as we shuffled quickly from line to line. Our buses had a Marine escort as we arrived at the airport for our 6:00 a.m. flight. It was strange, looking out from our bus at dawn as Liberians lining the streets waved to us, still smiling.

We walked toward the plane, and before I began climbing the steps I turned to take one last look at the rain forests and the people, and the gray, wet sky, and I felt the warm air on my shivering skin and smelled the wood burning, and for a moment I heard the children from Dada Town singing *Jesus loves the little children,* and pictured Paywon trying to keep the garden alive, his little body carrying a huge pail of water on his head, then pouring it slowly over the struggling plants.

Cameroon, West Africa

The Road to Doukoula

by Mary Beth Simmons (Cameroon 1989-91)

Standing on the side of the road in the tiny village of Bougay in Northern Cameroon, I watched as the driver of the mammy wagon—the freelance minibuses of West Africa—tried to figure out his next move. My fellow passengers and I were headed for a village called Doukoula. It was my first trip to the place I'd call home for the next two years as a Peace Corps Volunteer.

The road from Bougay to Doukoula had been washed out from heavy rains and would be difficult to navigate without oars. *"C'est une riviere,"* one old man sipping a beer told us. I looked at our driver and asked what he was going to do. He thought about it and decided he would go to Yaguoa. Everyone piled back into the wagon.

Everyone except me. Though my sense of direction in the wilds of Cameroon was vague at best, my gut told me Yaguoa was not where I wanted to go. I felt a strange burst of exhilaration and misplaced confidence and decided, instead, that I would leave the ragged security of the mammy wagon and hitchhike. The fact that I had never hitchhiked in Africa, or anywhere for that matter, didn't seem to matter. All I knew was that I had a friend in Kaele, only a few clicks toward the west. I could get a ride to her place and come up with a new plan in the morning. Sure.

A boy scrambled to the top of the mammy wagon and tossed down my bags—my life—packed with all the essentials for existence in Africa. When the man below failed to catch the bag that contained my cookware, the clatter and crunch of metal against the pavement was an omen of things to come.

The adventure of the Peace Corps, I thought, was going to begin once I had reached Doukoula. But there on the road in Bougay, it was already underway. The wagon took off, and as I heard the fading laughter of the passengers, I was sure I had done the wrong thing. No one else stayed behind to hitchhike. I paced there on the side of the road, occasionally pausing to stare down the long strip of asphalt shimmering with heatwaves, hoping my concentration would cause a vehicle to materialize.

Two hours passed without a single car. At the beginning of the third hour I plopped down on my overstuffed duffel filled with clothing, bed sheets and towels, and put my head in my hands. Two little girls who had been watching me from across the way scooted up and joined me there on the duffel. They sat on either side of me and offered a small, rusted tomato tin filled with groundnuts. I thanked them and ate the nuts. They giggled.

The distraction was welcome, but it couldn't divert me from my dire transportation straits. Every time I looked at my bags marooned in the dust, my anxiety level rose. I was sure I was looking at my bed for the night. As dusk began to fall, though, I heard the unmistakable sound of an internal combustion engine in the distance. Then I could see it, a dot that quickly became a battered old Toyota pickup. I flagged it down and begged the driver to give me a lift to Kaele.

Initially, he wasn't too receptive, but warmed up to the idea after I pressed a 5,000 franc note into his hand. I tossed my gear into the back of the truck and hopped up front with him.

Despite the Toyota's decrepit condition, the bad roads, and no lighting, the driver was doing 85 miles an hour. The engine was roaring, the windows were down and the wind was flying like we were on Harleys. All of a sudden, a rock came out of the twilight and shattered the windshield, spraying glass all over the front seat and us.

For some reason, the driver found the glass storm great fun. Laughing, he continued our Daytona-500 pace. The noise of the engine and wind was so loud I could barely hear myself speak. I yelled at the top of my lungs for the driver to stop. *"Il faut arreter!!"* I screamed. No response. I yelled louder. Still laughing, he finally pulled the truck over. I got out and brushed the glass off my pants and shirt and shook it out of my hair. In the side mirror I counted three nicks. Blood streaked my shocked expression. The driver couldn't stop laughing.

But when I leaned against the truck, removed my boots and windshield glass came pouring out of them, I laughed, too.

Peace Corps Volunteers are, in my view, as dedicated, hardworking,
and inspired as they were in the beginning. They represent for me
the best that is in us, living as they do in conditions of hardship,
overcoming obstacles many of us might not be able to face, and
making their own personal contribution to a better world.

Carolyn R. Payton
Peace Corps Director
1977-1978

Cape Verde, West Africa

An African Gift

by Diane Gallagher (Cape Verdi 1990-92)

It was midnight. The children of the village had been tucked under their protective mosquito nets, the cows were in their rickety corrals, the mother hens had pushed their chicks into hollowed-out places in the soft dirt, and the sound of sleeping Africans filled the air.

I had spent the day being ushered around by my host for the weekend and was exhausted by the effort of being up, friendly, responsive, and alert, and God yes, weary from trying to speak their language. Now it was night and the hugeness of the African sky lulled and calmed me, and I relived what had happened to me that day.

As part of our three-month training, each trainee was to spend a weekend with a host family in the interior. When our trainers first mentioned this exercise, many felt a little apprehensive; I was just plain scared. I was told I would be by myself and my host family would take good care of me. God, I could only hope so. They gave us a list of phrases in Crioulo, which is the local language, and as I looked at the letters strung together I wondered how in the world I would ever be able to be fluent.

N pirdi	I'm lost (might use that a lot!)
N ka na pirdi	I won't get lost (am sure I won't use)
In	Yes (that I can remember)
Es I ke	What's this?
Kila I ke	What's that? (but how will I know what they say when they reply?)
Diskulpa	I'm sorry (apology)
Koitado	I'm sorry (sympathy—they've got two kinds of sorry... uh oh)
N bin fala mantenha	I have come to say my greetings
N bin dispidi	I have come to say goodbye (we were told this would make everyone sad, so be prepared for long harangues and pleas to stay just a little longer)
Te utur bias	Till next time
Tchau	Goodbye (ha, I already knew that one!)
N tene prublema	I have a problem (with luck I will not have to use this one very much)

At this point, the words of advice a returned Peace Corps Volunteer named Kingman gave me came into my head: "Don't be afraid to make a fool of yourself; keep the ability to laugh at yourself with you at all times."

As we packed for our adventure I looked apprehensively at the few items I was bringing with me. A small bottle of bleach to treat my drinking water. A package of Gatorade, in case we became dehydrated. A rolled-up mosquito net, my Swiss Army knife, a cotton nightgown and my sandals—this was all I would need. The skirt and blouse I wore would be changed only once. Practicality was to be the order of the day.

Before going to our villages, three trainees and I were driven to pick up the president of the region. The first person we saw was a large woman coming down the broad cement steps of an impressive building. We were invited inside, where the favorite game played in Africa began, hurry up and wait. Men scurried in and out, talking with the woman. When she rose and told us to leave, I realized that she wasn't who I thought at first, the wife of the president; she *was* the president. The four of us piled into the falling-apart truck, the president in front, of course. Then much to my amazement, a group of young and old men climbed into the back with us. There had barely been enough room for the four of us. Now there were nine, and no one batted an eye. The springs groaned, the engine sputtered and we were off.

At each village along the way, a Peace Corps trainee was dropped off, the president making introductions and smoothing the way. The very last stop was the village which would be my home for the weekend. A crowd gathered, the president swung into action with the rituals of protocol, and then suddenly the truck and the president were gone. The man who had been introduced to me as the chief, Abu, bowed towards me and gestured for me to follow.

We walked towards a sturdy structure of dusty orange bricks all piled neatly in place and topped with thatch. Abu motioned to the room at the end of the hall. There was a huge double bed and a wooden bureau and the ever-present mosquito net. Small wooden stools lined one wall and a gazelle skin hung on the other.

This was to be my home for the next three days and nights. I unpacked my small backpack, took out my letter of introduction from our Peace Corps country director and gave it to the chief. The letter had the United States seal on it and it was praised by all the men who had, unobserved by me, slipped into the room and were now occupying the stools next to the wall. I took out the picture of my four children, paused a moment to let the homesickness pass, and put it on the bureau.

When the chief saw that I had finished unpacking, he asked me if I would like to take a walk around the village—at least I think that's what he said.

The village was fairly large, and the smell of wood smoke filled the air. Abu took me to meet the blacksmith, a short, stocky man with a pleasant smile. When I looked at the huge muscles on his arms I was awed. He nodded briefly and went back to his work, operating a bellows over a fire surrounded by pieces of metal, wood, and an audience of dozens of village people. I watched and asked permission to learn the bellows; he shook his head no. After Abu asked him in Crioulo, the blacksmith handed me the bellows and showed me how to use them. I was not good at all. Sweat began pouring down my forehead and the salt stung my eyes, but I was determined not to stop. Finally the fire was hot enough and he handed me a huge hammer. By now my arms were screaming for a cool bubble bath.

A piece of metal was put into my other hand and the blacksmith showed me how to hit it. Now I knew why his muscles had muscles. Wang! The reverberation went through both my arms. After what seemed to be hours, most likely five minutes, the blacksmith took the hammer and the thin piece of metal and smiled. He nodded to me to follow him into the jungle that surrounded the clearing.

The blacksmith grabbed a limb from a branch and started whittling, then gave me his knife and motioned for me to continue. The whittling almost finished me, but I hung in there until he told me by body language that it was done. He strode back to the clearing. I limped. He put the stick into the hole of the metal I had banged the hell out of and there it was, a real hoe. My God, Abercrombie & Fitch could not have done a better job. All the children smiled, Abu smiled and I shook hands with the blacksmith who had given me my first metal-work class.

Abu saw how tired I was and took me back to his home for a short nap. Later, after a long walk through several villages, a wonderful dinner, and great conversations about my life in the United States (which, with the help of miming and body language, they seemed to understand), Abu motioned for me to follow him out to the field. I went with complete trust, for he had sort of adopted me and treated me like a sister. It was now midnight and the stars were so brilliant it took my breath away.

In my mind, I reviewed the day as Abu sat quietly next to me. I remembered when a wild rainstorm burst upon us and we were forced to duck into a hollowed-out tree to shelter ourselves from the downpour. I thought of the brand-new baby, only hours old, that had been given to me to hold for good luck. Of the small Moslem temple where I was asked to write my name on their tablet, and of the lady who ran after me to give me a ripe banana. Of our village children with my white string on their wrists as bracelets, of the animals constantly surrounding us, and of the earth, productive and worn out at the same time.

And now it was midnight, and I looked up towards the full moon. Abu smiled at me and began talking in Crioulo about the stars. He gave their names and I listened in fascination to all the stories he told me about them. I then told him the English names and the stories I had been taught by my parents. The simplicity of the night and our comfortable conversation made me realize how very fortunate they all were to have a chief like Abu. An hour went by, he took my arm and we walked back to our homes in silence. I barely remember the process of getting into bed. No tooth-brushing for me that night.

The light of dawn reflecting from the orange clay bricks awakened me, and I could hear children's muffled cries, pots being filled with water, women cajoling babies, men coughing; all telling me that life and the day were beginning again in Africa. As I swung my legs out over the large bed, I felt something touch my feet under the sheet. I saw a huge banana leaf tied with a vine at the bottom of the bed. Picking it up gingerly, I untied the leaf and there was the hoe, the very hoe I had made the previous day with the blacksmith. He had come in the night with his present and I never heard a sound.

The Peace Corps has taught two generations of talented and highly motivated Americans (many young and some not so young) that splendid conundrum that lies at the heart of a good life: the more you give, the more you get.

Not only do most Volunteers have an experience that becomes the yardstick by which they measure the rest of their lives. But we as a nation are also reminded that our unique contribution to the human family is neither our wealth nor our economic system, but the tradition of volunteerism which flows like a mighty stream through every decisive moment of our nation's history.

Richard F. Celeste
Peace Corps Director
1979-1981

Swaziland, Southern Africa

Lomkhuleko and the Fine Coffee Table

by Sam Birchall (Swaziland 1991-93)

After two years of arguing with the School Committee of Elulakeni High School, in outback bushveld Swaziland, about whether it was useful for girls to take Woodworking Class, I won and soon found myself with six freshman girls among a sea of boys, bringing my class total to around thirty. Only one of the six girls was really fired up about our first project. That was Lomkhuleko, an otherwise shy girl, who rarely spoke in class.

To keep things simple, I had designed a small table. It stood about 14" tall. My usual deal was that a student had to get a grade of at least 80% on the basic table to be allowed to paint or varnish it. I issued wood, and we got to work.

Lomkhuleko had no developed woodworking skills at all. She had never ever seen anything made. The one thing she had in abundance was a dogged determination. The five boys who shared her workbench were pretty helpful, and she recut pieces several times in order to get the table assembled and freestanding. Though the table was not as level as it could have been, I was almost as proud of it as she was, as it squatted there in the front of the room with twenty-nine others, awaiting the grades. It always amazed me to see a large group of tables sitting around, and not a one the same height as any other, even though each had sprung from the exact same plan.

All of the students were excited about taking their tables home, and all of them were certain that they would get an 80% and would be allowed to paint them. During lunch period that day, I was looking over the tables, grading them, and Lomkhuleko came into the room to see if she could get started on painting her table. Having rendered a fairly nice table in spite of its being a first attempt, Lomkhuleko was awarded a grade of 88%. And since she had shown the initiative to come and check, I got out the various liters of different-colored paint so she could decide what color she wanted to paint her table.

Just then, a student came in and told me that the headmaster was asking for me. I gave Lomkhuleko a brush, told her to pick a color, and left for the office. The meeting with the headmaster lasted the whole lunch period, and I raced back to my shop to put away the paint before the next class came in. Lomkhuleko was still working, and I noticed that she had opened every one of the eight or ten cans of paint. My heart skipped a beat as I approached her bench, and I envisioned all the things that might explain why all those cans had been opened in order to paint one very small table.

To my amazement, I found that Lomkhuleko had taken small pieces of notebook paper, twisted them into a point, and had painted a detailed picture of the homestead on which she lived. She had even figured out how to use a different paper twist for each color, and had mixed small amounts of various colors to get the shades that she wanted. It was such a charming picture that I asked in surprise, "Have you ever painted a picture before, Lomkhuleko?"

"No sir," she replied, looking at the floor. "I have never

seen so many beautiful colors, and I wanted to make my table very beautiful. It is for my grandmother, who told my father to let me come to your class. He does not think that woodworking is a proper thing for girls to learn."

"How did you know to mix the colors so well?" I asked, looking at subtle browns and greens.

"I just tried my best, Mr. Maseko."

About two weeks later, I was sitting in a homestead with about a dozen of the community fathers, and they were telling me how pleased they were to have a woodworking program at the high school. Lomkhuleko's father was there also. I overheard him telling one of the men how proud he was of the "fine coffee table" that his daughter had made in the class, and how he was sure that she would develop into a "fine woodworker one day soon."

I have visited thousands of Volunteers around the world during my tenure as director. And I see the same stars in their eyes, the same dedication to service present from the beginning of the Peace Corps. Volunteers are indeed America's proudest boast.

Loret Miller Ruppe
Peace Corps Director
1981-1989

Lesotho, Southern Africa

The Cana Chicken Incident

by Gregory Knight (Lesotho 1992-94)

I never discovered why Cana Primary School moved its three hundred layer hens from the new chicken house to the standard four classroom, and to this day that bothers me. I had planned an easy Friday and the day started normally enough. The familiar pack of wild dogs woke me at five, and as I listened to the six o'clock news on the BBC, a tiny herd boy clothed in only a ragged shirt chased a black pig across my porch. A week earlier high school students had rioted and burned the local school, and at seven that morning I heard workers repairing the buildings.

"Ntate Thabo!" Three school girls waved at me through my hut's open door. They smiled and ran towards my house, where the tallest approached me and held out a folded piece of white paper.

"Ke lebohile," I thanked them.

"Buh-bye," they said in high-pitched squeals and ran down the hill.

The letter from the Peace Corps office in the capital had

been forwarded to me by my friend Mike two weeks before I received my own copy, but I read the short message anyway.

There is a Security Situation in Maseru. Remain at your sites and remember that travel restrictions are in effect. Do not visit other volunteers or travel to camp towns. Troubles may escalate, so listen to Radio Lesotho for further information.

Radio Lesotho had since been shut down by the army, so I dismissed the note and proceeded with my day's agenda as an agriculture technical advisor to primary schools.

I sensed something amiss when I approached the hen house and heard nothing. Complete silence seemed unnatural for three hundred chickens, so I stood on concrete blocks and peered through the steel-barred windows into the back of the stone building. It was empty. I thought that the red chickens had been stolen, or else removed by the teachers and students for de-licing. I proceeded into the school compound, where I heard squawking in a classroom, and through a dirty window saw the birds shuffling around on a thin layer of dead grass spread over the concrete floor. The nesting boxes remained in the chicken coop, so eggs—most of them broken with hens devouring the insides—dotted the classroom floor.

Two years in Lesotho had taught me never to seek reasons, but curiosity made me question the nearest teacher.

"Madam, why are the chickens in the classroom?"

"Yes." She smiled. "The birds are in the classroom."

"I see that, but *why* are they in the class?"

"I do not know. You must ask that one woman."

"Oh...that woman. Is she that side?" I pointed.

"Yes." The teacher smiled and counted money from the previous day's egg sales. I was getting nowhere, so I looked for the agriculture teacher responsible for the layer project. I found her and the other instructors in the absent head teacher's office huddled around a paraffin heater.

"Ntate Thabo! Hoa bata!" they said as I entered the closet-size room.

"Yes," I answered in the sixty-degree winter heat. "It is very cold today." I wore only a tee shirt and jeans but shivered for their pleasure, then got straight to the point.

"Madam, why are the hens in the classroom?"

"Yes, Thabo. The chickens are in the classroom." The largest woman answered and the others nodded in agreement.

"All right," I continued slowly. "Yesterday the chickens were in the hen house. Correct?"

"Yes," the woman answered again.

"Okay, good. Now, today, right now, the chickens are in the classroom. Correct?"

"Yes," she answered.

"Why are the birds in the classroom?"

"Yes, Thabo! The chickens are in the classroom."

"Madam, can you please come with me?" She nodded and followed me from the office up to the chicken coop and adjacent classroom. "Yesterday the chickens were here, right?" I walked over and stood next to the chicken house.

"Yes."

"But today they are here," I said, and walked to the classroom.

"Yes."

I breathed deep and then asked, "Why?"

"Yes, the chickens are there."

I panicked until hit by sudden enlightenment. I had it! "Madam, you are going to put the students in the chicken house!"

"No, Thabo." She shook her head at my stupid suggestion.

"So Madam, the building will remain empty?"

"Yes." She smiled as I hit the nail on the head.

"Madam, I am very confused. When the head teacher returns, will you tell him to visit me?" She nodded and returned to the school office. I entered my hut and waited until my counterpart (the woman teacher responsible for my sanity) appeared at my door with two trays of eggs.

"Thabo, these are for you from the school. Eat these when you are confused." I laughed and thanked her. "And Thabo, your friend Mike is here." Across the clearing Mike walked through the row of aloe plants that surrounded my house, and I remembered seeing a vehicle driving across the soccer field towards the school.

He began with an order. "Pack your stuff. We're out of here."

"What?"

"There's fighting in Maseru. They're evacuating us to a safe house. Grab your stuff. The van is waiting."

It took only a minute for me to pack and say goodbye to my counterpart. Mike and I each grabbed an egg tray and loaded ourselves into the already crowded van. The mini-bus drove past the school compound on our way out, and one of the other Volunteers noticed the chickens flying around the classroom.

"Greg, why are your chickens in the school and not the layer house?"

"Yes," I answered, smiling as if I knew all the answers to the question, why. "The birds are in the classroom."

The Cotton Trenches of Uzbekistan

by Beatrice Grabish (Uzbekistan 1992-94)

On the fifth day of "barf" (Tadjik for snow) in November 1993, the troops surrendered. The war, a.k.a. the cotton harvest, lasted eight weeks this year and yielded (only) 87% returns.

I had watched my students pile into a twenty-five-vehicle motorcade and wind around the mile-long university boulevard amidst handkerchief waving and cheers from teachers and other onlookers. Two days later, much to the horror and surprise of my women colleagues at Samarkand State University, I joined the students' work camp.

On October 5, I arrived at the collective farm called Guzelkent, about forty kilometers outside the city limits. The place was a collection of brown-streaked whitewashed houses made of mud brick, rising like Oz out of acre upon acre of cotton fields. It was a scene framed by purple mountain peaks and a flawless blue sky. The first day, I walked with a fellow *demlow* (Uzbek for teacher) through the cotton fields, trying to pick out my own students from brightly colored hunched-over backs.

My colleague's well-trained eye spotted them. "There they are," she said, "just like the enemy hiding." And there sat three Uzbek girls, their white kerchiefs bobbing at boll-level with the cotton stalks. The women looked like mummies as they picked the cotton, their mouths and noses wrapped with gauze. The men's faces were unprotected. Crop dusters disgorged defoliants which shrivelled the greenery and exposed the cotton for clean picking. A yellow residue remained on the cotton. Hearing the advancing buzz of the plane, I ran and hit the deck, covering my head. Everyone laughed and the *domla* reassured me that it was "only salt."

At lunch time the brigade assembled on the sidelines, huddling around a wood-burning samovar. One student was the designated "cooker" for the group, and spent the whole morning fetching water from the community well, gathering food, and mixing up a pot of potato or macaroni soup. Before eating, students weighed in their cotton, hooking their bulging aprons onto a wooden tripod with a sliding-rule scale. Each sack contained up to twenty kilos. (Students strove to meet a 100-kilo quota per day.) After the tally, the cotton was tossed onto a rising mountain and then picked up by a flat-backed truck and carted away. The *domlas* and collective farmers dined atop the cotton; the students sat on the ground sharing one bowl of soup among six and passing around a cup of tea.

I expected the students to grumble about the conditions, as I knew American students would. But instead of rebellion there was an overwhelming sense of resignation at the camp: the cotton was here to be picked, and we were there to pick it. University studies span five years instead of four, so the students can spend a full year picking cotton during their tenure. The government orchestrates the effort, and every night President Karimov appears on national television to read each region's returns like a roll call of war dead.

Students are quick to defend their Republic, saying that

Okotin (white gold, as cotton is known) is the only currency that Uzbekistan has right now. They pick for future generations. Picking is a rite of passage: their parents and grandparents picked, and so will they. For the collective farmers, I was the first American that they had ever seen, much less the only American to participate in this government agriculture campaign. Villagers peered at me, grade schoolers touched me to make sure I was real. One group of tenth-form students shyly approached me to give me a handful of walnuts and a piece of bread. *Mekmonlar* (guests) are treated with the utmost care and respect in Central Asia. My own students displayed their hospitality by giving me the thickest slabs of kielbasa and bread, though they had next to nothing to eat themselves.

I slept with nine of my fourth-year Uzbek girls in one room. At the end of the day, we dined on the bedroom floor. And after dinner, vanity ruled. Preening in hand-held mirrors, some girls rolled their bangs in curlers, others bridged their brows together with black paint. Some girls read, others knitted, and a few boogied to a boom box in the corner. I felt as if I had parachuted into a "Grease" slumber party, Uzbek-style. Boys were on everyone's minds. All of my students were to marry the following spring, though none knew their future mates.

Communal living was intense. My back ached, my skin burned. The squatton was located in a sheep stable out back. No baths, no gas, no beds. The students slept on collapsible cots, the same contraption that I mistook for a lawn chair in GUM, the department store in Samarkand.

Uzbekistan no longer belongs to Russia. My friend Ulugbek told me, "Our Republic is just a baby, and we must teach it to grow up." But cotton monoculture is firmly entrenched. Irrigation networks drain the feeder rivers to the Aral Sea, and cotton flourishes in a desert. University students pick it. I teach English. And so life goes on.

Perhaps we should not place as much emphasis on tabulating, measuring and quantifying Peace Corps' work. Using numbers to describe the work of Peace Corps may be as ineffective as trying to describe an impressionist painting by the number of colors and dabs of paint. We know Peace Corps has been successful the same way an artist knows she is successful. Other people admire her work.

In the Peace Corps, we have one of our nation's most potent and efficient empowerment tools. We empower people, transferring to them knowledge and skills to improve their own lives. We also empower nations. We have been a major empowerment force for the fledgling democracies born during the revolutionary years of 1989 and 1990.

Paul D. Coverdell
Peace Corps Director
1989-1991

Niger, West Africa

Trekking to the Sahara

by Deborah M. Ball (Niger 1992-94)

Dust swept across the yard into the eyes of crying babies and patient mothers. I picked up the next naked baby to weigh him on the scale. Before I could get out of his target range, he peed down my dress and legs. I gently laid him down on the scale. He looked at me and saw my strange white skin and alien facial features, and he screamed until he was back in the comfort of his mother's arms.

After many months of dusty yards and frightened babies, I needed a break from my community-health-care work in Niger, and thankfully, the group of fellow Peace Corps Volunteers with whom I had trained had planned to meet up for a camel trek. I traveled east for four days across sub-Saharan West Africa to find my friends. Niger does not have any trains, so the main form of long-distance transportation is by "bush taxies."

The vans were built to seat fifteen people, but the driver

interwove legs and arms in order to sardine twenty-five passengers, plus a few babies, into the broken seats. To get maximum use out of the space, he placed live poultry under the seats. Everyone wore flip-flops, and the chickens and guinea fowl pecked at our exposed toes. The cramped quarters did not allow for any shifting and the unpadded seats and smell of twenty-five hot, sweaty, unwashed bodies made for an arduous ride.

Since Niger is predominantly Muslim, we stopped five times a day for prayer call. Everyone piled out of the car and rolled out small bits of carpet, straw or plastic mats. They kneeled toward Mecca and went through a series of half-hour rituals involving bowing, standing, and praying. Then the taxi man drove on at hair-raising speeds. He wove his way in and out of the donkeys, goats, and camels that meandered in the road.

The driver made stops to pick up stray travelers or drop people off in places that seemed completely uninhabited. There are no service stations along the roads in Niger, but our driver stopped to pour gasoline into the tank from his storage canister. During refueling breaks, we made use of the natural bathrooms—one side of the road for the women and the other side for men.

Looking out the cracked window of the taxi, I could see across the stark, beautiful landscape. Herds of African cattle with elegant long white horns strolled together across land dotted with huge baobab trees. As we traveled east, the color of the majestic mesas, little mountains of wind-carved rock, changed from hues of deep red-orange to light pink.

On my journey, I had to go through forty-two military police check-points. Each road stop took at least an hour. All the luggage, elaborately tied down on the top of the taxi, had to be untied and lowered down. Military men holding semi-automatic machine guns searched all the passengers' bags. Some items, such as cases of beer, were sometimes confiscated for no apparent reason.

The military asked all of us for identification and interviewed each passenger. They enjoyed asking questions to the anasaras, or foreigners, in the group, particularly the women. I was often asked if I was married or single and if I would like a boyfriend or husband. In Niger the men buy their wives. I usually told the men my bride price was very expensive and quoted some outrageous sum of money that they could not afford. They laughed and enjoyed my mocking since they knew *anasara* men did not buy their wives.

I met up with some of my friends, and we continued the journey together. Twice our bush taxis reached the main cities late at night. Curfews meant we had to sleep in the taxi until morning, when the military would let us into the city. I had no warm clothes with me, so there were long, cold hours. The temperature went from 120 degrees Fahrenheit during the day to 45 degrees during the night. Some of us slept on the seats of the van and others slept on prayer mats next to or underneath the van.

The second time we had to wait to enter a city, my friends and I crowded around the bonfire the military guards had made. The guards were pleased I could speak Zarma (a West African language) with them. They asked about my journey and were surprised when they found out how far I had traveled. Though they would not let us across the border, they brought out a dirty mattress for us to sleep on as we waited for morning to come. My friends and I gratefully piled on it, huddling together to keep warm. The morning was signaled by the first prayer call, and then the military guards brought us to the police, who insisted that we register as tourists before they would let us into the city.

When we finally convened, our safari consisted of eight African guides, twenty-five fellow Peace Corps Volunteers, two Danish men, and six Frenchmen. Most of us were to travel by camel but a few in Land Rovers. We knew there was a war going on up north, and I was told that the rebels had shot a man on a camel twenty-three times with arrows. Our African guides were worried that we might encounter rebels, so they arrived prepared for the safari with bows and arrows.

The rest of us were a little less informed and a little more carefree. We wanted to experience cameling north into the Sahara.

After the initial difficulties of mounting protesting camels, we set forth for our safari. We hid from the harshness of the sun under colorful turbans. The rough wooden saddles had no padding and were painful. Bruises set in a few hours into the ride. Yet, I could not resist racing with the other two Volunteers who rode in front with me. The lopey, choppy camel's gait turned into a smooth-sliding trot and then a lively canter as I bounced around hoping that the rope holding the saddle on would not break and send me tumbling twelve feet down into the scattered thorn bushes and trees.

Our friends who rode out in four-wheel-drive Land Rovers conveniently met us on the way north and handed out cold beers to refresh us for the rest of our tiring, but beautiful, adventure. Finally, we reached the Sahara. Here the sand slips like an incoming wave over the vegetation of the saheil. We camped out next to the dunes, built a bonfire, and ate chickens that had been killed and plucked that morning. I helped give out our rations of French baguettes and wine. I savored everything that went into my mouth, as if I had starved for days.

The next morning, we woke up early and braved the cold to explore the dunes. The part of the Sahara we were in is called the Tall...which makes me think of the tall white flowing waves of the sand through which we waded. We scattered in all directions running, diving, sliding, and falling down the soft white hills. We tackled each other and rolled over with the sand filling our shirts and pants.

I took off my shoes and felt the gentle carpet of sand with my toes. I walked along the windblown cliffs that were such great fun to slide down. The contrast of the foamy white sand against the royal-blue sky grew sharper as the morning light broke through. I thought about how Niger is full of contrasting bitter and sweet experiences.

Czech Republic, Central Europe

Extended Families

by JoAnn Seibert (Czech Republic 1992-94)

Ernie, Harry, Gordon and I commuted for years together in the 1980's—two hours a day, five days a week in a faded-blue 1976 Honda Civic with a few hundred thousand miles on it. We figure we spent well over 2000 hours nestled together.

We listened to National Public Radio news and the traffic report and then turned off the radio, all of us preferring silence. Gordon always slept next to me in the back. Our legs were the shortest. Ernie drove and Harry and I read, worked or studied. None of us worked at the same place, so we could freely vent our frustrations at the end of the day—fifteen minutes each, and then we were home. We learned a lot from each other, too, as each of us had an entirely different profession. Eventually, Ernie, Harry and Gordon talked about their wives and grown kids. We all talked about ourselves and our pasts.

Ernie, we found out, spoke Czech before he spoke

English and still spoke it, but he had never set foot outside North America. He and his brothers and sisters grew up in the Czech-speaking Valach family in Montana, his father having immigrated to the States in 1910.

I excitedly called Ernie when I found out the Peace Corps was assigning me to what was then Czechoslovakia. He supplied me with a list of his Czech first cousins, none of whom he had ever met or spoken too. He also gave me the name of a Moravian village where his father was born in 1892.

One cool sunny day during my third summer in the Peace Corps, I went to that village, Rostín, near Kroměříz. The list of cousins I had from Ernie showed only Antonín Konecny in Rostín, with no address or telephone number. So I had prepared myself for finding no one, or for Antonín, if he were alive, not comprehending who in the world I was.

When I got off the bus, I spotted the town hall across from the bus stop. In Czech, I explained to the competent-looking, wide-eyed woman and young man in jeans in the office that I had a friend in Oregon whose father was born in Rostín in 1892 and had left for the United States as a young man. I timidly added that I was looking for my friend's cousin, Antonín.

It turned out that the man in jeans was the mayor; he knew cousin Antonín and everyone else in town. The woman opened a small card file and pulled out one of eight hundred tattered index cards—one per resident—and read off Antonín's date of birth and other vital statistics. I asked for directions to his house and, still a little worried about what the reception would be like, started out the door.

However, the mayor insisted on driving me in his own car. We pulled up in front of Antonín's house. No one was home but the dog was in the yard, a sign, according to the mayor, that they weren't far away.

Undaunted, the mayor continued to the family cottage on

the outskirts of the village, where he found not Antonín, but instead cousins Bozena and Liduöka. They were a bit surprised to see the mayor and even more surprised when he explained I was from Oregon and knew Ernie. They were confused until I figured out that Ernie was *Arnoöt* in Czech.

Once they made the connection, they all literally grabbed me, stroked my arms, wiped tears from their eyes, and hustled me into the cottage where Ernie's father was born. The mayor drove off.

I had planned to spend two hours in Rostín, which proved to be impossible. They send out word somehow that I was there, and from 11 a.m. that day until noon the next I saw cousins from four cities and a good number of Ernie's nieces, grand-nieces, nephews and grand-nephews. In my letter to Ernie I wrote, "Then we went to the 14th-century chapel on the top of a hill just outside the village. Next to the chapel is the cemetery where your aunts, uncles, grandparents and great-grandparents are buried. After coffee and Czech cookies at the cottage, we went to Antonín's house. His wife gave me a beautiful lace tablecloth she had made. I was a bit embarrassed and confused. I said I would take it to your family. She said, 'No, it's for you; they get one when they come.'"

After loading my day bag with canned and fresh fruit from the garden, cousin Liduöka saw me off on the train with *kolac,* a crystal vase and tears in her eyes, which she explained by saying that only one other time had someone from "America" come.

Ernie can speak Czech, but he can't read or write it. His relatives speak only Czech. They've never, ever communicated with each other in writing or by telephone—distance, elapsed time and the language barriers were too great.

Now, however, if all goes as planned, Ernie and part of his Oregon family will be visiting the Czech Republic in the near future.

Peace Corps Volunteers have the opportunity to make a real difference. One of the momentous events that occurred during my tenure as director was the collapse of the Soviet Union. World peace and stability hinged upon the orderly transformation of that region. Peace Corps was among the first aid programs requested by the newly independent states of the former Soviet Union. This story of Peace Corps assistance is repeated throughout the world. As director, I have seen the wonderful work of Volunteers, past and present, in my travels. The art of their handiwork is ever present.

Elaine L. Chao
Peace Corps Director
1991-1992

Holy Water in a Vodka Bottle

by Kevin O'Donoghue (Latvia 1993-95)

In Latgale, the region of Latvia where I served as a Teaching English as a Foreign Language Volunteer, Catholicism is the predominant faith. In the spring of 1994, I had the privilege of attending an Easter service there, in the village of Bernani. This is a town so small that most Latvians don't know it exists. It doesn't have a single shop, a school, or even a post office. In fact its only landmark is a 250-year-old Catholic church built entirely of wood.

The church itself is an anachronism, situated beside a cemetery against a backdrop of auburn rye fields where horses still pull the plows. One could only guess at how old its paint job is, the gray paint chipped and peeling in places. There are no stained-glass windows or statues of the saints. It's just a simple building off to the side of the road. Only its modest steeple and the cross on top distinguish it as a place of worship.

My hosts and I drove up to the church on a dirt road

scarcely wide enough for two cars and parked on a narrow strip of grass just outside the gate. There were only four other cars there when we arrived, and no one else was in sight. I later learned that the church doesn't even have its own clergy. A priest has to drive in from another parish every week for the service.

I didn't expect to find the interior of the place any grander than the exterior. But I was wrong. Once inside, I found it absolutely magnificent. Its most prominent feature was a hardwood altar stained a deep shade of mahogany and trimmed with gold. Behind the altar, Saint Mary and the infant Christ were depicted in silver. Paintings as old as the church itself decorated the walls, and colorful parish banners hung from long poles at the ends of the pews. Accompanied by a beautiful antique organ, a women's choir filled the air with sonorous Easter hymns.

One of the things that I noticed first was a perfectly normal aluminum bucket that had been placed near the wall. It looked as though the janitor had forgotten to put it away after scrubbing the floor. Later I saw an elderly woman, her gray head swathed in a scarf, approach the bucket and draw out a ladleful of water. Very carefully she poured the water into a small crystal vial she had brought with her. It was holy water. I thought it terribly odd that the church kept holy water in such an ordinary vessel as a bucket.

People continued to come into the church, one after the other, as we waited for the service to start. Many of them walked over to the bucket and filled some sort of vial or jar with holy water. It struck me as a very quaint tradition, setting out the holy water for people to come and take as they like.

One man entered the church, made straight for the holy water, and began ladling it into an empty vodka bottle. How could he do that? I found myself thinking. Holy water in a vodka bottle! What an obscene mingling of the sacred and the profane. Then I saw that part of the label had been removed, as if the man had realized that holy water doesn't belong in a liquor bottle and tried to scrape it off. He filled the bottle about halfway and then joined his family.

At first I was a bit shocked by what I'd seen. Then, I realized that it doesn't matter whether holy water is carried in a crystal vial, an aluminum bucket, or a vodka bottle—it's still holy water. Usually we try to honor the sacred with something more appropriate though. Churches of every creed and confession all over the world are filled with precious metals and priceless artwork. We who attend church dress up for it. We genuflect when we enter. People invariably pay the sacred a great deal of respect. It just didn't seem right to carry holy water in a vodka bottle.

As I sat there thinking about what I'd seen, however, the vodka bottle suddenly made sense. Latvia is not a country where people can afford to buy expensive crystal, let alone gold or silver. Most of the bottles that Latvians have are misshapen or discolored. But vodka is sold in clear, attractive bottles. These are the nicest bottles to be had in Latvia. This kind of recycling is very common there. When we think of recycling in America, we think of taking our bottles to a plant that processes them. In Latvia recycling means using something over and over again until it either breaks or finds some permanent niche in the home.

The more I thought about it, the more I liked the idea. It was a perfect symbol of Easter—taking something as profane as a vodka bottle and putting it to a more wholesome use. It was redemption.

There was one other surprise awaiting me that day. After the service, the family I was visiting in Bernani invited me back to their house for Easter dinner. It is a tradition among Catholics in Latvia to drink a small glass of holy water before eating dinner on Easter Sunday. So when we were all seated at the table, someone pulled out the holy water. My friends kept theirs in a vodka bottle as well. And we drank it, solemnly, with all the reverence that holy water deserves.

My Peace Corps experience in Guatemala thirty years ago was the most profound and eye-opening education I have ever had. As a Peace Corps Volunteer, you find out you're more adaptable, a little tougher, and more resilient than you thought.

Carol Bellamy
Peace Corps Director
1993-1995

Honduras, Central America

Goods and Services

by Larissa Zoot (Honduras 1993-95)

For a couple of weeks I was content to sit and wait patiently, watching the light bulb flicker on and off. At first it took ten minutes, then twenty, thirty, forty-five and finally it would be over an hour before the connection was made and the light stayed on in my room. When it reached one hour, I lost my patience and just didn't bother turning it on anymore.

I got by this way for several weeks, going to bed early or hanging out at the neighbors' instead of spending the evening in my unlighted house. Getting ready for bed only took a few minutes and it was easy to do by candle light. I had lived that way for six months before the electricity came, so there was no reason why I shouldn't have been able to keep living that way.

Then something strange and unexpected happened. I began having a lot of work to do, more work than I could finish before the sun went down in the afternoon. Electric light became a necessary resource so I had to track down an electrician.

The "electrician" turned out to be a young newlywed who lived just down the street. He showed up at my door late one afternoon with a screwdriver and a roll of electrical tape and started taking things apart. I'm sure he had no training or formal knowledge of electrical systems, so I held my breath, crossed my fingers, and tried to be of use, handing him parts when he needed them and otherwise staying out of his way.

That evening he could not find the flaw or fix it, but he came back early the next day. This time he took a few more things apart, found the problem, and fixed it. Once he had the light fixtures put back together and I had tested it several times to make sure it worked, I smiled contentedly, following him to the door, and asked the standard question: "How much do I owe you?"

The reply I received was also standard. "Nothing. Just your thanks." No money. No goods in trade. Not even a beer or a soda. Just thanks. So I offered him my most grateful, enthusiastic "Thank you!" and then watched him disappear down the street.

This is something I've experienced many times now in Alubarén, and it always leaves me stumped. Doesn't he realize that what he just did for me is considered work? Doesn't he know that his time and effort have value? Doesn't he need every penny he can get to provide for his new wife and baby?

Obviously he's not aware that back at home in the United States I would have paid through the nose for the services of an electrician or for any other work I needed to have done. Is it possible that he doesn't recognize that I'm one of the highest paid people in this town overshadowed by poverty, and I would gladly hand over whatever amount he chose to request? Or does he realize all of this and it's me who's missing the point?

I think over some of the other times when I've experienced this phenomenon...

♦ the bus driver who hauled my new furniture over from the next village when the Volunteer there left

♦ the seamstress who took in the waists of my shorts when I lost too much weight and they were falling down

♦ the carpenter who carried my new bookshelf down the mountainside on his back

♦ the mayor's secretary, who typed up an official letter that I needed to send to the Ministry of Health

♦ the teacher who took my packages to the post office on her weekend in the capital

♦ the neighbor who lets me cook on her stove any time I want to, but won't ever let me buy her any more firewood.

And there are more. What is it with all of these people who are so kind and do so much for me, but never accept any payment or ask for anything in return? Is it because I'm the gringa, an outsider, and they want to give a good impression of their people and their country? Do they intend to create that good impression by treating me extra special?

That's what I thought at first, but with time I realized that I'd been mistaken. It seems to have been another case of my seeing things through the filter of my North American values.

Now I've been in Alubaren long enough to gain a truer perspective on how things work here. The bus driver runs errands for people all the time and never charges a penny. A person who has coconuts or mangoes growing in her backyard will give them away to a neighbor who doesn't have them, but needs them for a recipe, and not even expect a sample of the finished product. A seamstress will stay up all night long making school uniforms for the children of another mother who doesn't have a sewing machine. Its just the way they are.

I hope that this generosity, this sense of community, is something I'll be able to take back with me. I hope I can remember it and practice it, at least to some extent There's something very special about a place where the primary "value" placed on goods and services is the people's value for one another.

The Peace Corps is one of our nation's most valuable assets. Its value is rooted in both the ideals it represents and the tangible impact that Volunteers have on the lives of people in developing countries. Peace Corps Volunteers reaffirm the importance of American ideals and the spirit of altruism. They unite the dream of a better world with the will to make it happen.

Mark D. Gearan
Peace Corps Director
1995-present

Swaziland, Southern Africa

Abundant Rewards

by Laura Stedman (Swaziland 1994-96)

One day in science class, we were reviewing the topic of the animal cell. The students had memorized what they needed to know to pass the national standardized exam, and for that I was pleased. But I couldn't help feeling that something was missing. Where was the spark? They dismissed and shied away from my requests for their opinions. The students refused to offer their own possible explanations for experiments and observations. Instead, they wanted to know what the 'right' answer was. They didn't seem to consider that there were mysteries and secrets of nature, that there was more to know than what the examine cared to test. I asked myself: "Do they recognize the magnificence that takes place here in the cell? Why don't they share their thoughts? Do they understand the topic? Do they care?" I was frustrated because I felt that I was unable to really reach them.

I was having doubts about teaching until I found a diagram in the back of one my students' notebooks. This diagram changed my perspective on teaching. In her notebook, the student had drawn the unlikely comparison of an animal cell to a Swazi homestead. She had given the grandmother of the homestead the role of the nucleus. The mitochondria, the organelle which supplies energy to the cell, was represented by the sisters.

I called her into the staff room and asked her to explain what she had written. At first she thought she was in trouble. Then she started to open up. She explained that she had given the grandmother the role of the nucleus because 'grandmother decodes when and how things get done."

As she continued I began to see that she had indeed understood the intimate workings of the cell. I was proud of her, and I told her. "But Miss," she said, "I don't know why you're happy. I only did this from my own mind to help me understand this better."

"I know," I said. "That is why I am proud of you."

I began to understand that young men and women need confidence in themselves and their own worth, as well as direction for their critical thought. With this in mind, I changed my teaching methods to encourage not just academic achievement but also emotional growth. Something magical started to happen in that class. Students started to see themselves as having worthwhile opinions and were not afraid of sharing them. I saw students taking risks in their ideas and growing from them. I felt truly honored and privileged to be part of it.

My love of teaching is genuine. Teaching provides a unique opportunity to learn something new from young people while guiding them toward their goals. The work is challenging and the rewards abundant.

Kyrgyzstan, Central Asia

Fingerprints

by Craig Redmon (Kyrgyzstan 1995-96)

After almost a year in Kyrgyzstan, we were still treated as honored guests. In this Central Asian republic one dramatic mountain range collides and boosts itself upon the back of the next until the entire country rises in a riot of glaciers, rivers, and peaks. The Kyrgyz people, once nomadic, are famous for their open and genuine hospitality. It came as a shock to everyone when Kate and I were robbed.

It was late May. We swung our door open to find books and papers strewn about the floor. Drawers dangled, and a hot wind poured over Jalal-Abad's scorched pistachio hills and through the balcony window our thief had punched out. We staggered about the apartment numbering our losses. After a few minutes, I collected myself and ran downstairs to find the police.

Two and a half hours later, the investigation began with the arrival of four pairs of Kyrgyz detectives. We solemnly shook hands in the entryway. They made an immense pile of their black, vinyl shoes by the door, lit cigarettes, and produced pads, pens, clipboards, and dense forms for us to fill out. The fingerprint specialist burst into action, dusting every item our thief may have fingered, including walls and table legs. The gold hammer and sickle shone brilliantly from his cap, both epaulets, and the badge over his heart, even though the Soviet Union had broken up into independent states almost five year ago. The specialist only paused when he spotted Kate's green REI headlamp which the thief had miraculously overlooked. He was spellbound.

"I'll have to dust this carefully for fingerprints back at the station," he said, turning it over in his hands. I asked him when we could pick up the headlamp. *"Patom,"* he said and stuffed it into his bag.

Then the investigation moved into the questioning phase. What kind of clothes were stolen? How many pairs of shoes were stolen? Why do you have so many pairs of shoes? There were also cultural questions. Do you enjoy eating our national dish? Does Michael Jordan live in Los Angeles? By now the fingerprint specialist had discovered my cracked and warped Russian guitar. He plunked at it thoughtfully. One of the detectives suggested that Kate and I sing a song. I had been watching Kate's frustration mounting, and at the song request she burst.

"There's no time for singing," she shouted, "we've been robbed!"

But the detectives assured us that they had plenty of time. So, in the interest of moving the investigation along I played and Kate harmonized on a rousing rendition of "You Are My Sunshine" to the immense pleasure of our guests. An hour later the detectives closed their notepads and snuffed their cigarettes. They sorted out the pile of shoes by the door, promising that justice would be served. We didn't see the detectives again until late summer.

On September 21, there was a knock at our door. One of the detectives stood in the hallway smoking. I shook his hand.

"We caught your thief," he said, flicking the spent cigarette down our stairwell. "His name is Vitaly Andreavich. He is your neighbor." He told me the case would now go to court and that the judge requested my presence. I asked him if the fingerprint specialist would be returning Kate's REI headlamp now.

"Oh," he said, lighting another cigarette, "Detective Rostomov has retired. The trial date is set for the fifteenth of October. Come to court then."

The courtroom was in disrepair. Chairs with missing backs stood in uneven rows before a battered deposition stand. A young Russian man I understood to be Vitaly Andreavich leaned in the aisle handcuffed and smoking. Another much older, haggard-looking Russian man sat in the front row near a window with warped glass. He wore a well-patched suit, and when we shook hands I noticed his eyebrows were caught in a high, expectant arch. I took a seat next to him.

A few minutes passed before the judge entered the courtroom flanked by the defense attorney and one of our detectives. The judge was a sharp-looking Kyrgyz man with wisps of hair swept back on his head. He wore a blue and white polka-dot shirt with long, starched lapels. He walked with a book and a thick stack of folders clamped in his left hand. Also, his right arm was missing, the empty sleeve tucked neatly into his belt. He took a seat behind the bench and fished out a pair of glasses from his shirt pocket.

"This case, number 144 part three and four, will be tried in the usual manner," he said. "Anyone at any time can ask a question of anyone else in the courtroom, is this clear?" He motioned for me to stand. "There are two men who may have seen your robbery from the alley, but they are in the village and won't be present today. Should we continue without them?" he asked. I said I thought all possible evidence was important for a fair trial. The judge nodded judiciously and said, "We'll continue anyway; tell your story."

I related everything I knew about the robbery, what was

stolen, and our time spent with the detectives. When I finished, the judge barked, "Questions!" The courtroom remained silent. The judge smacked his one meaty palm on the bench and said, "Vitaly Andreavich, stand and tell your story." Vitaly described getting drunk on vodka, tying a rope to a pipe on the roof, swinging over the edge and through our window. He showed how he had lowered our things to the ground and then climbed back up the rope to the roof. The old man with the eyebrows nudged me and whispered, "This kid's got a pumpkin for a head." When Vitaly Andreavich finished, the judge asked if there were questions, this time without looking up. Silence. He struck the bench with his one hand and said, "Part four."

The old Russian man beside me stood and told his story. He described drinking wine on a Tuesday night with his girlfriend and Vitaly Andreavich. He and his girlfriend had gone out on the balcony to smoke a cigarette when Vitaly crept into the kitchen, hefted a large bowl of honey from the counter, ran down the stairs, out into the street, and sold it to someone walking by. The courtroom erupted. Vitaly Andreavich flew to his feet, booming and shaking his handcuffs. Vitaly's previously mute lawyer pounded his table. The judge was standing now. His empty right sleeve had worked itself loose of the belt and swung carelessly back and forth. He raised his powerful left arm for order, and when it was restored, he said, "I will render a judgment in thirty minutes. Dismissed," and smacked the bench.

We waited in silence. Vitaly and the old man smoked. I looked around the courtroom and accidentally made eye contact with Vitaly Andreavich. He raised his handcuffed hands, pointed his cigarette at me and said, "I'm going to write you a letter from prison, but after you read it you must tear it up." I leaned forward and began nodding when the judge entered. We all stood. The judge easily balanced a huge, open record book in his one hand and read.

"According to the laws of Kyrgyzstan, it is the judgment of this court that Vitaly Andreavich receive six years in prison for robbery plus an additional year for the theft of the honey." He looked over the top of his glasses. "However, I have taken it upon myself to suspend this extra year." He slammed the book shut and said, "Case closed." I never saw the old man with the eyebrows, the one-armed judge, or Vitaly Andreavich again.

This spring I opened the door to find one of our detectives smoking in the hallway. He asked me if we'd had any more trouble since the robbery a year ago and inquired as to our health. He said he'd been trying to catch us at home because he wanted to give us something. He reached into his coat pocket and pulled out Kate's green REI headlamp. "As it turned out, we couldn't use it as evidence. Anyway, all the fingerprints were ours," he said.

Colombia, South America

Twice In My Life

by Maureen Orth (Colombia 1964-66)

My Medellín has never been like the headlines that have been flashing round the world for a decade. The gentle "city of eternal spring," the capital of the department of Antioquia, that I lived in and cherished for two years in the sixties as a PCV, has been morphed into a violent and bloodthirsty symbol of illicit drug-dealing—where bombs and kidnappings have replaced conservative Catholicism and the Antioquenos long-held reputation for entrepreneurial fervor.

Today the rap on Medellín is horrendous: the U.S. State Department warns Americans that all of Antioquia is off limits for safe travel. Journalists are especially susceptible to guerrilla attack. My Colombian *novio* of long ago, who had become a Senator, was murdered in 1989 when he refused to give in to a self-styled militia leader who wanted a piece of his land. Amid this turmoil I could only dream of going back to Medellín to visit my Peace Corps site and to see the school that I had helped build.

My memories, of course, were vivid. One Sunday a dramatic posse of five men on horseback dressed in black *gaucho* hats and traditional wool *ruanas* galloped up to my door in the barrio. They were leading an extra horse for me. We rode straight up into the mountains for about three miles to meet an isolated community of *campesinos* in a *vereda* called Aguas Frias. The people were desperate for a school.

Several Sundays later we began with a community work day and formed a human chain to throw rocks down the mountainside to clear the land. A year later there was a brick building that on dedication day bore a crude hand-lettered sign that was a happy surprise to me: *Escuela Marina Orth*.

I had not seen the school since 1979. Then suddenly an invitation came out of the blue from "Friends of Colombia," our in-country group, and I thought that I must go. In the fall of 1995 I became part of an official goodwill tour of Colombia, one of a dozen former Colombia Peace Corps Volunteers graciously invited by the Colombian Ambassador to visit four cities. Medellín was not on the itinerary, but I could easily go there by myself. Things had calmed down, I was told, since the world's most notorious *narcotraficante,* Pablo Escobar, had been killed.

Then a curious thing happened: I became afraid of the depth of my own emotions. I couldn't even think of going back to Medellín without choking up inside. So many intense memories of specific people and the majestic, sweeping Andean countryside came flooding back—not to mention the Spanish language, the music, the freedom of galloping on a horse through grass as high as my shoulders. Of course in those days we called the rain forest the jungle; there were families of fifteen and twenty children, and good girls still courted through grilled windows; the young man wasn't allowed inside until he had declared. What if what I now saw broke my heart? We all knew the culture minutely; we had such a strong sense of identification with a country completely different from our own, and I was so young then, yet, never afraid of anything—not of living alone in a barrio considered rough, not of the rigid power structure that I believed kept my poverty-stricken neighbors locked in a dead-end destiny, and certainly not of the Peace Corps rules and regulations. The arrogance of youth—just leave us alone to do our work.

About a month before I was due to arrive, I wrote to the *Señora Directora* of the school at *Aguas Frias* and had an old friend who lived in the city deliver it for me. She could get there by jeep, my friend reported—the road was now paved and a horse was no longer required.

I didn't even recognize my old barrio, *Las Violetas*. Where once you had to cross a creek with water coming halfway up the bus's wheels to enter, today the creek is gone and the barrio, even more teeming with people and cars—cars!—looks not poor anymore but typical of a Colombian blue-collar neighborhood—an extension of a more prosperous area that used to be a few miles away.

As we climbed the road it was reassuring to see the towering Andes flanking us. The higher we climbed, the calmer I felt. At least the dark green mountains hadn't changed. And then we turned a curve and the day became magical. Two smiling, scrubbed little school boys in brand new uniforms were out on the road to greet me waving paper Colombian flags.

We parked below and they ran ahead to lead me up the steep steps (another innovation) to the carved-out mountain where we had built the school. "Here she comes!" they cried. At the top of the steps, in tears and hiding her face in her skirt, was my kind neighbor from across the street in the barrio, Doña Mariela—mother of fifteen, grandmother of forty, now widowed, now living close to the school. I too began to cry as I hugged her, the first of many tears that day.

The school looked fantastic. A second story had been added, hanging pots of tropical flowers were suspended from the upper corridor, and just below on the front wall was a big metal sign donated by a local soft drink company that said *Escuela Marina Orth*. Next to it hung a second, hand lettered sign: "Welcome Home." Instead of the 35 students in two classrooms that I knew of in the sixties, there were now 120 children in grades one through five. I was amazed and unprepared for the six-hour homage to come.

Slowly and shyly, men and women I had known and worked with came from around corners and behind pillars to greet me. They brought me lemons from their garden. They told me of births and deaths and invited me to their houses. I was most thrilled to hear that some children from the school had gone on to the university and were now professionals working in Medellín, a nearly inconceivable dream when we began. They exclaimed at and eagerly grabbed pictures of my family that I had brought to show them.

Then I saw Luis Eduardo, the humble, soft-spoken president of the vereda's community action junta and really the co-founder of the school as well. A portrait of us taken together nearly thirty years ago, now tattered, was brought out for our inspection. How many times Luis Eduardo and I had ridden to town together to knock on doors in the city government to beg for bricks and mortar. He was so quietly persistent that he had been hired by the city of Medellín to work in its office of school construction, a big step up for his family.

The children, shined up bright, were taking their places outside to raise the flag and sing for me the Colombian and Antioquenan anthems. The principal presented me with a beautiful homegrown arrangement of orchids, lilies and roses, and gave me a formal speech of introduction. With the children standing at attention, she announced a twelve-act program in my honor to be followed by a lunch, a serenade, a toast, and a mass!

I was standing but I felt I should sit. The moment was surreal. It seemed that I could almost touch the other side of the mountain. The populous valley of Medellin was spread out below and I was surrounded by these beautiful children honoring me in a school that bore my name. Was I really in this exotic place on this cool sunny Friday morning so far away from the rest of my life? I missed my family and wished they could share this with me. Nevertheless, I felt completely at home.

At the end, mass in this setting was simple and moving, celebrated by a young priest in white vestments on a makeshift outdoor altar in front of the school.

The mass to me was the most important part of the day. The people's faith remains strong and as a Catholic myself I felt a special bond in sharing it with them, in having the children come up to touch my hand to wish me peace, and to take communion with them.

I tried to make my fifth speech of thanks and told the congregation that the whole idea of the Peace Corps was to plant the seed so that the community could go on as they had. This was my real thanks—that they had persevered. As I turned to go I realized that at least once in my life, when I was young, enthusiastic and just doing my job, I actually accomplished something that my country and my family could be proud of. And twice in my life, the Peace Corps and the people of Colombia had given me more than I could have ever imagined.

Eritrea, Horn of Africa

Teaching Hope

by John Rude (Ethiopia 1962-64)

The setting, both exotic and familiar, matched the strange parade of emotions that passed through me as I met my former students for the first time in thirty-two years. We sat beneath an African corrugated metal roof, surrounded by bougainvillea vines in the backyard enclosure of a private club. The bright, late afternoon sun and cool highland air teased my memory, as did the faces of the middle-aged men who sat in a circle, trying to recall what it felt like to be a ninth-grader. This was the perfect Eritrean moment that had visited me so often in dreams over the years—and like a dream, I knew the moment would rush by, then vanish.

In truth, we had to conduct the ritualized greetings almost as strangers.

Only a few of the sixteen faces were vaguely familiar, and I'm sure they could recall very little of my youthful teaching persona—perhaps the sound of my voice, or a random gesture. I thrilled silently to hear the sound of names that I

had learned to say during daily roll-calls: Kebrom...
Woldegabriel...Tareke...Mebrahtu...Berhe... The names of
other students rolled off our lips, former students who could
not be here now because they were busy, or were living on
another continent, or had been killed in the war with
Ethiopia and now lived only in memory. I had heard how a
few of them died, some as fighters in the war of liberation,
others as fleeing refugees. But I did not know how those
gathered here had lived, and this was the moment of discovery.

In all places and at all times, teaching is an honorable but
odd profession. You stand before a class and impart knowledge
you are not sure that you really possess. You pass frantically
from exam to exam, dipping into your students' minds
in a structured, artificial way to measure what they might
have learned, what you might possibly have taught. Your
own personal crises are forgotten in the classroom, a place
apart, where the teacher and students must always be ready
to perform.

You can never learn enough about your students, because
there are too many names and faces to remember, too
many scores to record. The scores become numbers in time-
yellowed books that are eventually discarded; so many of the
individual students pass into the blur of memory. If your
teaching had results, you try not to think about what those
results might have been. In your heart, you carry always the
nagging doubt that your reading, your writing, your dramatic
acting, precise measuring or passionate caring made little difference
in the lives that passed before you.

As I stared into these faces in the African twilight, I knew
that, for me, there had been results. We laughed as a few of
these distinguished men recited the dialogues I had once
forced them to memorize, thinking at the time they might
retain the dialogues for a week. We joked about "Peace Corps
English," the spare, carefully-enunciated language we
American teachers had used in order to make ourselves
understood. All could now comfortably communicate in this

international language, and for this my students were grateful.

But the more significant result was in the professional lives these students had lived. I could not claim to be the cause, but I was astounded to hear the one-sentence recitals of their achievements. "I'm with the Teacher Training Institute," the first one explained, condensing his life of dedication to resurrecting the quality of teaching in Eritrea's schools. "I'm with Haddas Eritrea," said the next—no, not just "with" the newspaper, but an editor. "I'm with the Defense Ministry," said a third, modestly omitting the fact that he was a high official, and had just returned from specialized training abroad.

Many of those gathered said, "I spent some years in the field"—shorthand for twenty or more years of guerrilla fighting in rugged trenches. These men had survived one of the most brutal and ignored wars in recent history, and they were proud of their role in winning it.

I was proud simply to have known these men in their impressionable youth. If along with their parents, fighting comrades and political leaders, I had contributed to their hope for a better future in Eritrea, then it was even better, for that hope had sustained my former students through the fires of a hellish war.

We laughed together in the clear Eritrean twilight, but I knew that a gulf of more than years separated us. I had come from a country rich in material wealth and touched their lives briefly a generation ago. They had stayed in Eritrea to fight for its freedom. Now the roles had reversed—I was the student, they were the teachers.

Or perhaps this was the relationship all along, and I was belatedly discovering it. Teaching is full of surprises, but I knew this was a moment I had spent a lifetime preparing myself for, and it had finally arrived.

A Zen saying came incongruously to mind as I sat with my students in the bougainvillea twilight: "When the student is ready, the teacher will come."

Nigeria, West Africa

Finding Boniface

By Martin Gleason (Nigeria 1961-63)

I returned to Nigeria in 1981 after an absence of eighteen years. My trip was sponsored by the American Participant Program of the United States Information Agency. When my official duties, which had kept me in the northern and western parts of Nigeria, were completed, I headed toward the East. My mission was to find an old friend I had lost touch with, or at least to find out what happened to him.

Some things had changed in Nigeria since I was first there. But the important things—the look of the land, the warmth of the people, and the ambiance of black Africa—were the same. There were more cars, buildings, roads, power lines. City streets still teemed with people. Travel and lodging were still a challenge. Americans were still welcome, but there seemed to be less interest in foreigners because Nigerians were preoccupied with the struggle to build a nation.

When I arrived in Nsukka with my Peace Corps group in 1961, one of the first Nigerians I met was Boniface, a cleaning man in the dormitory where we were housed. Boniface was the first member of his family to leave the village of his ancestors to live and work in a modern setting. He and I became acquainted, even though at first it was difficult to bridge the class barriers that Nigerians seemed more conscious of than Americans. Boniface became my interpreter of Nigerian life. He was as decent, honorable, and industrious a person as you could find anywhere. And he was a pilgrim on a journey he might not have been quite aware of: from subsistence farmer to urban proletarian to—someday—a middle class burgher who could educate his children so "they won't have to go through what I went through." That's a familiar story to Americans, but in the kaleidoscope that was Nigeria it happened, not over generations in the life of a family, but in the life of one man.

After I left Nigeria in 1963, Boniface and I corresponded regularly and shared thoughts on matters large and small, especially those dealing with work and family. I was asked for advice on the qualities a young Nigerian should look for in a wife. I tried to provide career counseling to an ambitious young man without many marketable skills who was trapped in a situation where jobs were few and advancement was not always based on merit. In spite of obstacles, Boniface persevered. Then came the Biafran War and there were no more letters from Boniface. What had happened to Boniface? I wondered whether the war had taken him.

In 1981, I told the story of my long-lost friend to the steward of the house in Enugu where I was staying. He agreed to make inquiries about this Boniface. That night he spoke to some friends on the university staff in Nsukka. He learned that Boniface had been in the civil war, but that he had survived and returned to work in the university. He did not know where or in what department he worked.

I arranged for a car and driver and the next day traveled the forty miles to Nsukka. My old stomping ground, the

University of Nigeria at Nsukka, was barely recognizable. It had been a large, raw clearing in the bush, a cluster of dun-colored buildings surrounded by dust storms in the dry season and mud in the rainy season. Now it was a green and well-groomed campus with a network of paved roads and the orderly demeanor of institutional middle age. Opened in 1961 on the outskirts of a tiny crossroads town, the university was now surrounded by a thriving commercial center. The school, brainchild of Dr. Nnamdi Azikiwe, had obviously been a great economic catalyst.

After several leads proved fruitless, my driver located a friend of his who knew people who worked with the first Peace Corps Volunteers eighteen or nineteen years earlier and who agreed to help us find Boniface: "The man must be found—God wills it."

By then it was 2 p.m. Saturday and I was due to leave Enugu the next day. The man who was leading our posse rounded up two friends who liked Americans and thought they might know this man Boniface. Our search party of five now proceeded to check out a place where my local friends thought Boniface had once lived. He had moved. We tried another location. No luck.

At the third stop we were told a man named Boniface lived in the compound with his wife and four children. A little searching produced Boniface's wife, somewhat suspicious and frightened. At first she said she didn't know where Boniface was, but after a heart-to-heart talk in Ibo she said he was "on his farm." After fifteen minutes' drive into the bush we found a yam patch and a bicycle leaning against a tree, but no Boniface. Shouts of "Boniface" brought no response. Then we saw the head of a man peering out from behind the tree. He took a long look at me, let out a yell, and jumped straight up in the air. I had found Boniface!

Over several bottles of Star beer we got reacquainted. Seems the U.S. Postal Service had returned two of his letters to me marked "addressee unknown." He had been to war. He had also married and begun to raise a family. He was still on the support staff of the university, something of a record for employment in Nigeria's uncertain economy. Boniface's family lived in essentially one room. There was no electricity and the water tap was a few hundred yards away. His major project in the last several years had been to put his savings into the construction of a ten-room building in Nsukka that would one day house his family in a few rooms and supplement his wages by leasing the others. The adobe walls had been up for a couple of years, but inflation and other vicissitudes had halted progress. Now the rains had begun to take the walls down. The structure needed a roof or it would be a loss. After some discussion of the cost of "zinc" (a.k.a. a "bam bam" roof) I decided Boniface needed a silent partner willing to invest a few dollars in a good man and his dream.

Boniface's seventh child, born in 1988, is named Martin. This was the second attempt, this time successful, to name a child after me. (The first time the priest ruled that "Gleason" is not a Christian name.)

Today, Boniface and his family live in four rooms of a ten-room dwelling near the center of Nsukka. Six rooms are leased to paying tenants who enjoy the "luxuries" of running water and electricity. Boniface is still scratching to make ends meet but he does have a chance to educate his children. Like most of us he's got a mortgage of sorts. And me? I've got an old friend back and a little piece of Nigeria to boot.

Venezuela, South America

Since You Leave, Nothing is Like Yesterday

by Judy Harrington (Venezuela 1965-67)

Our first year in the Peace Corps, my former husband Ken and I developed a YMCA site in Los Haticos. When we transferred to the YMCA Training School in Caracas, Bob and Elaine Joyce replaced us, enlarging the program base and working with the same neighborhood youngsters from 1966 to 1968. We wrote to people in Los Haticos for a couple of years, then stopped. But not a year went by without Elaine and me saying: "We've got to go back." Twenty-seven years later, we did.

Sabado, 24 de Septiembre, 1994 We didn't know what to expect. We had sent a list of names to the director of the new downtown YMCA so he could *buscar a los muchachos.* Look for the boys. We also sent the list to Juan Jaume, our former neighbor. He connected with Roger Perozo, one of our kids, now a public relations director at the *Universidad.* Roger, together with Recortado, another of our boys, who now drives a taxi, spread the word that we were coming. But we did not know what to expect. We only knew that Jaume was expecting us.

On this anxious Saturday morning, at the YMCA *parque,* one of our old YMCA leaders, Rafa, arrived and embraced me; I was crying just at the sound of his name. His bear hug was so sincere: We had waited many years to see each other again. A pain had stayed in his heart, he said. The embraces just kept coming...Eloy, Robinso, Lexie, Bella, Americo, Alberto, Colombia. The young man who had felt like a son to me, Jesus "Chuito" Martinez, was in the army in Caracas. Johnny was dead. Oscar was a national soccer player. Henry was a con man. His brother Jairo was gay. On and on...

For hours, on the porch of Sr. Chacon's house, where we had lived as Volunteers, and in the salon of the YMCA, more boys showed up—Contreras, then Sutherland, then Solano, then Pera. So many of the boys we still only knew by nicknames. We were calling forty-year-old men names like Mr. Freckles, Pants, Shorty, Speed, Skinny Dog, and Tiger. Elaine showed our old slides. How these boys had changed and how they had stayed the same. It was wonderful!

The new director from downtown—Negrete—then started a little program for us. He had the "boys" share their *recuerdos de nosotros* (memories of us). Clearly one of their strongest memories was of our discipline and how many times they had been thrown out of the park for misbehavior. The infractions were written down on the back of their membership cards. Even though the Los Haticos YMCA was now devoid of programs and without a director, we managed to find a rubber-banded stack of 1960s attendance cards in a bottom desk drawer. The deeds and discipline were duly recorded...*groserias, luchando, tirando piedras, falta respecto.* They play-acted the fights and the consequences. They talked about our work changing their lives, giving them discipline, hope, and achievement.

The YMCA presented us with plaques and great little talks. My reply was *"Para mi parte, digo que mi corazon esta lleno de recuerdos.* [For me, my heart is full of memories.] We have been talking of this trip for more than twenty years, and it is a *milagro* that we made it. Thank you for your welcome, your love, and for remembering us all this time."

That evening I walked around the neighborhood with Americo and Mercedes, who were children when I was a Volunteer. As we strolled, Americo said his mother was still alive and lived in the same house. We walked up that street, and as I entered her small swept yard, a scene rushed back to me. Americo and Wilmer had been real favorites of mine when they were eight-year-olds. I took them with me on errands and trips as often as possible. But we always went to ask their mothers' permission. So this night, I asked Americo's mother: "Do you remember when I would come here?" "Si, si," she said. "To take Americo. But first he had to put on a clean shirt to go with the profesora!"

Later that night there was a *fogota* (bonfire), and more testimonials. One was from Jose Contreras, who arrived with a folder containing every scrap of paper he had ever earned at the YMCA: certificates for volleyball, for soccer, for his junior membership, his senior membership. He said, "Many people would give everything they have to go back to the way it was for us twenty-seven years ago." Then, gesturing to the fire, he said that one stick alone will soon burn out, but together they have great impact, great force.

As we all said good-by that night, Eloy sobbed in my arms. Mercedes was speechless through her tears. She looked as if she were in pain, and that matched my heart. Sr. Chacon, to whom I had given a Peace Corps T-shirt in the afternoon, said: "When you come again in twenty years I will have this shirt!"

Weeks after returning to the United States, we received a letter.

Dear Professors Roberto, Elena, y Judit,

I want to give you this short letter that I wrote for you last night. I would like to speak in the name of all the people (kids) who had the pleasure to know you. We are very proud to have you as teachers, guides in our childhood. We remember you as very important people that took place in our lives.

Since you leave, nothing is like yesterday. We always remember you in daily conversation. We kept your memories in our heart because you teach us with love. And when you give love, you receive the same thing—LOVE.

I am telling you what old people around the YMCA feel, expecting to see you again.

Sincerely your,

Helves Alberto Contreras ("Mr. Freckles")

Washington, D.C.

My Favorite Volunteer

by Theodore C. Sorensen

John F. Kennedy often invoked the old saying that "success has a hundred fathers and failure is an orphan." He would be the first to acknowledge that the Peace Corps, one of his proudest achievements, had a hundred fathers: a bill by Hubert Humphrey, a speech by James Gavin, an article by Milton Shapp, the example of the Mormons and a dozen other religious organizations, a petition from Michigan University students responding to his impromptu midnight challenge, and dozens of others.

This child first took breath, I'm proud to say, a few days before the Presidential election of 1960 in a campaign speech in which I had a hand, a speech on world peace in San Francisco on the night of November 2, when nominee Kennedy called for "a Peace Corps of talented...men and women, willing and able to serve their country" as teachers or engineers or doctors or nurses in developing nations around the globe. This proposal entered the official national agenda in his first State of the Union Address as President on

January 30, 1961, when he called for "the formation of a National Peace Corps, enlisting the services of all those...who have indicated their desire to contribute their skills, their efforts, and a part of their lives...to help foreign lands meet their urgent needs for trained personnel."

Thirty-five years ago today (March 1, 1996), less than four months after he first launched the idea in San Francisco, it became a reality. On the same day that he sent to Congress proposed legislation to establish a permanent independent agency, President Kennedy—unwilling to wait for Congress to act—exercised his own initiative and authority (as he did on so many occasions) and established the Peace Corps by Executive Order, thereby enabling it to be organized, fully operational and in the field by the time that bill passed six months later.

He wanted to get it underway before its detractors gained ground. And there were detractors. Many in the opposition party opposed it. Many liberals demeaned it. Many conservatives dismissed it. Many Communist governments denounced it. The Agency for International Development wanted to control it. The CIA wanted to use it. Leaders in some neutral nations, even those most in need of help, heaped ridicule upon it.

But John Kennedy and Sarge Shriver persisted. They persuaded. They prevailed. The legislation and appropriation passed the Congress; and each year of his Presidency the number of Volunteers increased; the number of countries served increased; and the President's pride in his creation, in these ambassadors of American idealism, increased beyond all measure. He took every opportunity to meet with returning Volunteers and to sing their praises to others. Tragically, his time for pride and pleasure in this epitome of the "New Frontier" spirit—like his time in office—was all too short. After his death, Peace Corps members in some countries were called "Kennedy's children." And I feel that all of you, all one hundred and forty thousand of you, are truly Kennedy's children.

But the Peace Corps' real history lies not in the story of its birth but in the story of its life, not in the archives of the White House or Capitol Hill but in the deeds of its Volunteers, in their fulfillment of President Kennedy's original mandate. History asks not why or how the Peace Corps was established, but whether it has succeeded, and whether its founder's expectations have been realized. I know no better way of answering those questions than to compare the words of my favorite President with the words of my favorite Peace Corps Volunteer, to compare the hopes of the original dreamer with the experience of one who is living out that dream today.

"We will only send abroad Americans," said President Kennedy "who have a real job to do — and who are qualified to do that job." They would, he had made clear on that November night in San Francisco, be "well qualified through rigorous standards, and well trained in the languages, skills and customs they will need to know...not only talented young men and women but Americans of whatever age who wish to serve the great republic and serve the cause of freedom."

Last July, my favorite Volunteer described her sixty fellow trainees in Morocco: "friendly, smart, funny and, of course, adventurous...with a real sense of solidarity...and extraordinarily diverse backgrounds and skills. The majority are twenty-something, but there are a couple of thirty-somethings, fifty and sixty-somethings, as well as a seventy-something...also a blind Volunteer—talk about courageous!" Later that same month she wrote: "It is so exciting to put my knowledge of Arabic to real use... Training is very intense—four hours of language and two hours of technical training every day, six days a week (for ten weeks)... My job will consist largely of counseling rural Moroccan women on maternal and child health, including family planning, a job that I not only care about but that I think I can accomplish." And in November she wrote from her site: "Yesterday, I vaccinated babies all morning. Earlier today I gave my presentation on diarrhea and oral rehydration…and the conversation evolved into a discussion of nutrition. This afternoon I gave a presentation about the merits of breast feeding… I really felt I was doing my job."

"I am convinced", said John Kennedy in San Francisco, "that our men and women in this country of ours are anxious to respond to the public service, are dedicated to freedom, and are able…to join in a worldwide struggle against poverty and disease and ignorance."

In this spirit, my favorite Volunteer wrote last August: "Life here…is hard by American standards—there is no electricity or running water, the health center…is insufficiently supplied…and large number of women give birth at home, without ever receiving prenatal care." And last September she wrote: "An eleven year old girl, Aziza, stops by my house a couple of times a week; today her mother wanted me to come for lunch. I observed how sickly her one-year-old sister looked, and the mother informed me that the little girl had diarrhea. I returned to the house after work with packets of oral rehydration salt."

"Life in the Peace Corps," said President Kennedy on March 1, 1961, "will not be easy. Men and women will be expected to work and live alongside the nationals of the country in which they are stationed—doing the same work, eating the same food, talking the same language."

Last July, my favorite Volunteer wrote about "the wind from the Sahara, a scorchingly hot, dry wind that blows constantly, rendering daily life like life under a blow dryer!" The following month, spending a week with a local family as part of her training, she wrote: "The family I live with is great…the father is a farmer of sheep and olive trees, and full of questions about the USA. The mother has shown me how to bake bread in a pan over a fire, and how to milk their cow…and has said that she will cry when I leave tomorrow." Then in November she wrote: "Winter arrived in the desert. There is a chill which not even the warmth of the ever-present sun can dispel. In a house that is virtually the great outdoors, many layers of clothing are a must. The desert climate is harsh, no matter what the season might be." And still later that month she wrote: "the weather is cold, but people are fortified by harira, a thick soup, for both breakfast and dinner, with couscous or tajine (a stew) at lunch, and multiple cups of tea and coffee...in the past five days I have eaten meals in seven different homes."

"But if the life will not be easy," said my favorite President on March 1, 1961, "it will be rich and satisfying. For every...American who participates in the Peace Corps...will know that he or she is sharing in the great common task of bringing to man that decent way of life which is the foundation of freedom and a condition of peace."

True to his prediction, my favorite Volunteer wrote as early as August about a presentation she had made on family planning that she felt had been a great success. "About ten women gathered and they were full of questions and very interested. I really felt like I was doing my job, and that this was why I was here." In September, on site at last, she wrote: "I don't believe how much I have learned in a week! I have distributed the pill and instructed women on how to use it; weighed new-borns; visited homes of women who did not come in for their pills; and gave the oral polio vaccine to hundreds of babies." After a brief Thanksgiving break, she wrote last November: "I'm glad to be back in Tinzouline. I now feel what two months ago seemed nearly impossible: that this is my home." And in January, after bringing her services to a nearby village, she wrote that it had "neither running water nor electricity, but its inhabitants are generous and friendly. I arrived not knowing a soul but left feeling as if I had many new friends." One month ago today she wrote about her observance of Ramadan, about her fluency in Arabic, and about the meals she shared at sundown with so many families, concluding once again: "In short, I feel at home...(signed) Your loving daughter, Juliet."

I am proud of my daughter. I am proud of my small part in the establishment of the Peace Corps. I am proud of this and other legacies left by the President I loved and served, John F. Kennedy. And I am reminded that his speech in San Francisco concluded with one of his favorite perorations, invoking Archimedes' words in explaining the principle of the lever: "Give me a fulcrum, and I will move the world."

Washington, D.C.

At Home in the World

by Bill Moyers (Deputy Director 1961-63)

Sometimes the soundtrack of memories deep in my mind begins on its own to play back the Sixties, with the echoes intercut by the incongruities of those years.

I hear the sounds of crowds cheering and cities burning; of laughing children and weeping widows; of nightrides, nightmares, and napalm; of falling barriers and new beginnings and animosities as old as Cain and Abel.

I hear the summons that opened the decade—"Let the word go forth"—and I hear the melancholy lament that closed it. "The stone was at the bottom of the hill," wrote one young man who had given his heart to three fallen heroes: "The stone was at the bottom of the hill, and we were alone."

But something survived those years that bullets could not stop. An idea survived, embodied in the Peace Corps Volunteers who are now 140,000 strong and still coming. This idea survived the flawed stewardship of those of us who were its first and amateur custodians. And it survives today. This is a testimony to the power of the idea.

Of the private man John Kennedy I knew little. I saw him rarely. Once, when the 1960 campaign was over and he was ending a post-election visit to the LBJ Ranch, he pulled me over into a corner to urge me to abandon my plans for graduate work at the University of Texas and to come to Washington as part of the New Frontier. I told him that I had already signed up to teach at a Baptist school in Texas while pursuing my doctorate. Anyway, I said, "You're going to have to call on the whole faculty at Harvard. You don't need a graduate of Southwestern Baptist Theological Seminary." In mock surprise he said, "Didn't you know that the first president of Harvard was a Baptist? You'll be right at home."

And so I was.

So I remember John Kennedy not so much for what he was or what he wasn't but for what he empowered in me. We all edit history to give some form to the puzzle of our lives, and I cherish the memory of him for awakening me to a different story for myself. He placed my life in a larger narrative than I could ever have written. One test of a leader is knowing, as John Stuart Mill put it, that "the worth of the state, in the long run, is the worth of the individuals composing it." Preserving civilization is the work not of some miracle-working, superhuman personality but of each one of us. The best leaders don't expect us just to pay our taxes and abdicate, they sign us up for civic duty and insist we sharpen our skills as citizens. Furthermore, to the extent that we are saved each day from the savage heart still alive within each of us, we are saved by grace—singular grace: the touch of a warming spirit, an outstretched hand, a spirit opened to others, a life generously shared.

Public figures either make us feel virtuous about retreating into the snuggeries of self or they challenge us to act beyond our obvious capacities. America is always up for grabs, can always go either way. The same culture that produced the Ku Klux Klan, Lee Harvey Oswald, and the Jonestown massacre also produced Martin Luther King, Archibald MacLeish, and the Marshall Plan.

A desperate and alienated young man told me in 1970, after riots had torn his campus and town: "I'm just as good as I am bad. I think all of us are. But nobody's speaking to the good in me." In his public voice John Kennedy spoke to my generation of service and sharing; he called us to careers of discovery through lives open to others.

Henry David Thoreau said, "I love a broad margin to my life." Most of us do but seldom achieve it. By stoking our imagination, John Kennedy opened us to broad margins. The theologian Karl Barth was five years old when he first heard the music of Mozart. It would delight him all his life. In 1955 Barth addressed a letter to the long-deceased Mozart, thanking him for all the pleasure of the music—all the pleasure and discovery. "With an ear open to your musical dialectic," wrote Barth, "one can be young and become old, can work and rest, be content and sad; in short, one can live."

The music of discovery. It was for us not a trumpet but a bell, sounding in countless individual hearts that one clear note that said: "You matter. You can signify. You can make a difference." Romantic? Yes, there was romance to it. But we were not then so callous toward romance. The best Volunteers waged hand-to-hand combat with cynicism, and won. They kept winning, until today the Peace Corps has earned a reputation (to quote the Washington Post) as one of the world's most effective grassroots development organizations.

The idea was around. It was in the air. General James M. Gavin, the wartime hero, had called for a peacetime volunteer force to be started as an alternative to military service. Senator Hubert Humphrey was preparing legislation for a youth corps. Congressman Henry Reuss and Senator Richard Neuberger of Oregon had cosponsored a Point Four Youth Corps. But it took a President to embody the idea, for the word to be made flesh. The Talmud tells us that "in every age there comes a time when leadership suddenly comes forth to meet the needs of the hour. And so, there is no man who does not find his time, and there is no hour that does not have its leader." Perhaps. But the wait can sometimes seem interminable, and we may miss the leader if the hour is late or we are weary and do not hear the music. John Kennedy was right on time with his idea. And we responded: Catholics, Christian Fundamentalists, Jews, blacks, whites, from every part of the country, from all economic levels, from various and sundry backgrounds: skiers, mountain climbers, big-game hunters, preachers, journalists, prize fighters, football players, polo players, enough lawyers to staff an entire firm, and enough Ph.D.s for a liberal arts college.

What was the idea that summoned us? Out of my own Peace Corps experience came a small gift from Albert Schweitzer, a framed and autographed picture which to this day reminds me of Schweitzer's belief in "the affirmation of life." He defined this as "the spiritual act by which we cease to live unreflectively." It was said that the urge to join the Peace Corps was passion alone. Not so. Men and women, whatever their age, looked their lives over and chose to affirm. To affirm is the thing. And so they have—in quiet, self-effacing perseverance.

They come—these men and women—from a vein in American life as idealistic as the Declaration and as gritty as the Constitution. I was reminded of this the other day when I interviewed the octogenarian dean of American historians, Henry Steele Commager. Reviewing the critical chapters of our story, he said that great things were done by the generation that won independence and then formed our government. Great things were accomplished by the generation that saved the union and rid it of slavery. Great things were won by the generation that defeated the fascists of Europe and warlords of Japan and then organized the peace that followed. And—said Dr. Commager—there are *still* great things to be won...here at home and in the world.

So there are. But if we are to reckon with the growing concentration and privilege of power; if from the lonely retreats of our separate realities we are to create a new consensus of shared values; if we are to exorcise the lingering poison of racism, reduce the extremes of poverty and wealth, and overcome the ignorance of our heritage, history, and world; if we are to find a sense of life's wholeness and the holiness in one another; then from this deep vein which gave rise to the Peace Corps must come our power and light.

The idea? Herman Melville got it right. We Americans are not a narrow tribe of men. We are not a nation so much as a world. And these Volunteers have shown us how to be at home in the world.

Listen to writer Michael Ventura: "The dream we must seek to realize, the new human project, is not 'security,' which is impossible to achieve on the planet Earth in the latter half of the Twentieth century. It is not 'happiness,' by which we generally mean nothing but giddy forgetfulness about the danger of all our lives together. It is not 'self-realization,' by which people usually mean a separate peace. There is no separate peace...Technology has married us all to each other, has made us one people on one planet and until we are more courageous about this new marriage—our selves all intertwined—there will be no peace and the destination of any of us will be unknown. How far can we go together—men and women, black, brown, yellow, white, young and old? We will go as far as we can because we must go wherever it is we are going *together*. There is no such thing as going alone. Given the dreams and doings of our psyches, given the nature of our world, there is no such thing as *being* alone. If you are the only one in the room it is still a crowded room. But we are all together on this planet, you, me, us; inner, outer, together, and we're called to affirm our marriage vows. Our project, the new human task, is to learn how to consummate, how to sustain, how to enjoy this most human marriage—all parts, all of us."

America has a rendezvous it has scarcely imagined with what my late friend Joseph Campbell called "a mighty multicultural future." But we are not alone and the stone is not at the bottom of the hill. We have Peace Corps guides—140,000 Volunteers who have advanced the trip. They have been to where our country is going. Out there in the world, as John F. Kennedy might say, is truly the new frontier.

'wideness' of the world came home to me vividly in Korea, and I've been exploring the world ever since."

Living in another country and speaking another language also taught these writers to think in these languages if they really wanted to understand what was happening around them.

"When I went to Korea in 1967," recalls Richard Wiley, winner of the 1986 PEN/Faulkner Award for _Soldier In Hiding,_ "My world was configured by the grammar of English and I believed, without having ever thought about it, that everyone else in the world saw 'things' just as I did. As I started to learn Korean I began to see that language skewed actual reality around, and as I got better at it I began to understand that it was possible to see everything differently. Even my opinions, on the same subject, were sometimes altered by changing languages. Reality is a product of language and culture, that's what I learned."

Poet Susan Rich, who was a volunteer in Niger recalls, "My world view developed and solidified during my years as a volunteer. That is to say, the notion of honor and respect towards 'the other', an innate curiosity towards exploring 'differences' (for lack of a better term), and a belief that the world was designed for me to discover, were already a part of my life pre-Peace Corps or I wouldn't have signed on for two years in Africa. My experience showed these ideas to be true and confirmed that there is a definite place for me in the world beyond home. My question is not what do Peace Corps writers share but simply how can anyone who wants to write not jump at the chance to become a Peace Corps Volunteer?"

The Peace Corps experience, as novelist and Micronesian volunteer P.F. Kluge, phrased it, "stretched our view of the world and then focused it, mightily precisely."

The experience was also intensely educational. The late novelist, Maria Thomas, said of her time in Ethiopia, "it was a great period of discovery. There was the discovery of an ancient world, an ancient culture, in which culture is so deep in people that it becomes a richness."

Novelist Marnie Mueller, author of *Green Fires,* a novel about Ecuador which won the 1995 American Book Award from the Before Columbus Foundation, says, "it made me more embracing of other cultures, and has given me all my richest material as a writer."

It was going to this dramatically different place that helped them become writers. Melanie Sumner, wrote her first novel, *Polite Society,* about Senegal, where she served as a Volunteer. Her novel won a Whiting Writers' Award for 1995. Novelist Mary-Ann Tirone Smith wrote her first book, *Lament for a Silver-Eyed Woman,* about Cameroon, her Peace Corps country. Mark Dintenfass used Ethiopia as source material for his comic first novel, *Go Make Yourself an Earthquake.*

Poet Ann Neelon found in Fatick, a small town in the bush country of Senegal, "an echo chamber for the cultivation of my own poetic voice. All day long, I spoke to myself in English; I spoke to everyone else in French or Wolof. Somehow, in doing this, I discovered a space that was inviolable, mine and mine alone."

P.K. Kluge wrote about Micronesia in his first novel, *The Day That I Die.* Three novels later, he returned to Micronesia to write about the islands and the death of a close friend who'd become President of the Republic of Palau. This account of his return, *The Edge of Paradise: America in Micronesia* is non-fiction, creative non-fiction. What this suggests is that literary forms change, markets change, writers change too—but some of these Peace Corps writers are walking around with a life-long connection to a place somewhere that is, and is not, home.

Whether it is prose or poetry, the Peace Corps experience is giving these Volunteers their literary territory. As Bob Shacochis summed up in an essay that appeared in *The Writing Life,* a collection of essays and interviews by National Book Award winners, "I know now that my novel *Swimming in the Volcano* would never have been written were it not for John Kennedy and his vision of the Peace Corps, his belief in the altruism and the fundamental goodness of Americans."

We are through our writings enriching America. When one looks at the books being written by returned Peace Corps writers, it is striking how many of them are winning major book awards and claiming space on literary bookshelves. The former Volunteer is coming of age as a literary person. We are telling the stories of the Peace Corps, and more importantly, of life in the developing world. A world that Americans know so little about, or care to consider.

We were not born early enough to be writers in Paris during the Twenties, or old enough to write the great World War II novel, but at last, thirty-five years after it all began, there is emerging a genre which might best be called Peace Corps Writings.

Perhaps this is a small claim in the world of literature, but it is ours alone to make. And it will be through our writings that we will create a place for the Peace Corps experience in the minds of Americans. We are bringing the world back home with our prose and poetry.

ABOUT THE CONTRIBUTORS

Deborah Margaret Ball (Niger 1992-94) was a nutritionist in Niger, where she administered the developmental status of malnourished children, and recruited and trained health care workers. Ball has a B.A. from Denison University. She is currently a candidate for an M.A. in Anthropology at the University of Hawaii at Manoa and a Student Affiliate at the East-West Center.

Andrew Scott Berman (Togo 1967-69) taught Mathematics at College Chaminade, a secondary school in Lama-Kara, Togo. He also worked in Benin in the anti-smallpox campaign. Berman has a B.A. in Mathematics from Queens College and an M.A. in Engineering from the University of Illinois. He currently works as a Telecommunications Engineer at Bell Laboratories.

Sam Birchall (Swaziland 1991-93) was a woodworking teacher at Elulakeni High School near Mbava, Swaziland. He also worked at Water Development projects and pre-school rehabilitation. Birchall has a B.A. in Economics and Administration from Wilmington College in Ohio.

John Coyne (Ethiopia 1962-64), founded with Marian Beil RPCV Writers & Readers, a newsletter for and about Peace Corps writers. Author of over twenty novels and books of non-fiction, he is the editor of *Going Up Country, Travel Essays by Peace Corps Writers*. At present, he is the Regional Manager of the New York Peace Corps Regional Office.

Paul Eagle (Liberia 1988-90) was a fisheries volunteer in Liberia, where he worked with local farmers turning swamps into swamp rice and fish ponds. He has a B.A. in Communications and English from California State University, Chico. After four years at a marketing agency in San Francisco, he currently works at Peace Corps headquarters in Washington, D.C.

Diane Gallagher (Cape Verdi 1990-92) was a small business development consultant on the island of Sao Vicente, working with the Minister of Housing and the Minister of Finance. She has an A.A. degree in Theatre Arts from Colby Sawyer, and a B.S. in Organizational Behavior from Lesley College.

Martin Gleason (Nigeria 1961-63) taught law and social sciences and helped establish Nigeria's first law school at the University of Nigeria at Nsukka. Gleason holds law and political science degrees from Loyola University and has pursued a career in government and public affairs in Washington, D.C.

Beatrice Grabish (Uzbekistan 1992-94) was a Teaching English as a Foreign Language (TEFL) Volunteer in Samarkand, Uzbekistan, where she taught English at the university level, started an information consulting center, and translated a book of local legends. Grabish graduated from Georgetown University with a B.A. in English Literature in 1991 and completed the Radcliffe Publishing Course in Cambridge in 1995.

Camilla Griffiths (Jamaica 1985-87) was a teacher/play leader at the hospital in Kingston, Jamaica. She also taught sewing at a school for adolescent mothers. Griffiths graduated from St. Olaf College, has an M.A. from Brown University and taught high school biology for 19 years. Griffiths and her husband, who also served in the Peace Corps, are now living in Charlottesville, Virginia.

Jacqueline S. Gold (Cameroon 1987-89) was a community development Volunteer in Dscang, Cameroon, where she helped women's groups organize community fields and soap-making cooperatives. Gold has a Master of Journalism from the University of Minnesota and a B.A. in Rhetoric and History from the State University of New York at Albany. She works in New York City as a financial journalist.

Orin Hargraves (Morocco 1980-82) was a TEFL Volunteer in El Hajeb, Morocco, where he taught English in the local high school. Hargraves has a B.A. from the University of Chicago, and is the author of *Culture Shock! Morocco, A Guide to Customs and Etiquette*.

Judy Harrington (Venezuela 1965-67) was a community development Volunteer and has had post-Peace Corps careers in journalism, political campaigns, and public administration. In 1993, Harringon, a Nebraska native, joined the Peace Corps again as Associate Director for Volunteer Support.

Charles Kastner (Seychelles 1980-81) was a physical education teacher in Victoria, island of Mahe, Seychelles, where he worked with physically challenged and mentally challenged children and adults. Kastner has an M.S. in Environmental Biology from Hood College and an M.B.A. from Pacific Lutheran University.

Gregory Knight (Lesotho 1992-94) worked as a technical advisor in agriculture and food production for seven village primary schools in Cana, Lesotho. Knight has a B.A. in English from Boise State University, where he will earn his M.A. in English, in December 1996.

Matt Losak (Lesotho 1985-88) taught English at a small mission boarding school in the central mountain range of Lesotho in southern Africa. Losak holds a B.A. in English from Southern Connecticut State University. He is the Public Affairs Officer in the New York Peace Corps Regional Office.

Bill Moyers (Peace Corps Staff/Washington, D.C. 1961-63) was an associate director and deputy director of the Peace Corps. He then became special assistant to President Lyndon B. Johnson. He left the government in 1967 for a career in journalism.

Maureen Orth (Columbia 1964-66) is a special correspondent for *Vanity Fair*. Orth has also written for *Vogue, New York Woman, Newsweek,* and *New West* magazines. She earned a B.A. in political science from the University of California, Berkeley, and holds an M.A. in documentary film and journalism from the University of California.

Kevin O'Donoghue (Latvia 1993-95) was a TEFL volunteer in Preili, Latvia where he taught high school in a rural community as well as started a non-profit educational publishing house. He has a B.A. in English from the University of Notre Dame and is pursuing a Master's degree in journalism at Northwestern University.

Craig Redmon (Kyrgyzstan 1995-96) taught English and literature in Jalal-Abad, Kyrgyzstan. Redmond, a poet, has a B.A. in English from the University of Idaho and does development work in the Kyrgyz capital of Bishkek. He served in Peace Corps with his wife, Kate.

Susan Rosenfeld (Senegal 1977-81) was a TEFL Volunteer in Joal where she taught junior high school in 1977-78. She then became the Volunteer leader for the TEFL program, working in the Peace Corps office in Dakar to train. Senegalese English teachers at the national teacher-training college. Rosenfeld has a Masters of Teaching English to Speakers of Other Languages from Teachers College Columbia University and a B.A. in Latin and history from Dickenson College. Rosenfeld lives and works in Niamey, Niger.

John Rude (Ethiopia 1962-64) was an English teacher in Tessenei and Mendefera, Eritrea. (Eritrea, an independent nation since 1993, was in confederation with Ethiopia in 1962 and was annexed by Emperor Haile Selassie while he was there.) Rude has a Ph.D. in Education from the University of Oregon, a M.A.T. from Oberlin College and a B.A. in history from Whitworth College. He visited Eritrea in 1995 as a consultant to the Ministry of Education.

JoAnn Seibert (Czech Republic 1992-94) has an M.A. from Colorado State University and a TESOL Certificate (Teaching English to Speakers of Other Languages) from Portland State University. Her Peace Corps assignment was teaching English at the university level.

Mary Beth Simmons (Cameroon 1989-91) was a TEFL teacher at Doukoula High School. Her writings about her Peace Corps service have appeared in *The Sun, Chile Pepper, Escape,* and the anthology *Traveler's Tales: A Woman's World.* She is currently living in Iowa City, Iowa working on her M.F.A. in Non-Fiction Writing.

Theodore C. Sorensen served as Special Counsel to President John F. Kennedy. Since 1966 he has worked as an international lawyer in New York City. He is the author of a half dozen books, including *Kennedy,* (Harper & Row, 1965) *and The Kennedy Legacy* (Macmillian, 1969). His youngest daughter, Juliet, is currently a Peace Corps Volunteer in Morocco.

Laura Stedman (Swaziland 1994-96) was a math and science teacher in a small village in Swaziland. She earned a B.S. in biology at St. Michael's College in Vermont and completed her service in the Peace Corps in January 1996. While traveling in South Africa on her way home to Maine, she died in a swimming accident. Her fellow Volunteers in Swaziland are planning to build a trail in a local nature park in her honor. It will be called "Laura's Trail."

Andrew L. Thomas (Rwanda 1988-90) was an agricultural research and extension Volunteer stationed at the high-altitude Rwerere station of U.S. Agency for International Development's Farming Systems Research Project in Rwanda. He holds a B.S. in horticulture from the University of Missouri and an M.S. in agronomy from Iowa State University. Thomas is presently coordinating rare plant conservation projects for the Center for Plant Conservation in St. Louis.

Moritz Thomsen (Ecuador 1965-67) was an agricultural expert in rural coastal Ecuador. He wrote articles about his experiences in *Living Poor, A Peace Corps Chronicle*. After his Peace Corps years, he lived and farmed in Guayaquil, Ecuador, where he died in 1991.

Larissa Zoot (Honduras 1993-95) was a child survival Volunteer in Alubaren, Francisco Morazan, Honduras, where she worked with midwives, volunteer health workers, and community groups in seven villages. Zoot is currently working on a Masters of Public Health in health management and policy at the University of Michigan, and has a B.S. in community health education from the University of Wisconsin at LaCrosse.

PEACE CORPS HISTORY

October 14, 1960 Presidential candidate John F. Kennedy addresses students at the University of Michigan in a 2 a.m. impromptu speech challenging them to give two years of their lives to help people in countries of the developing world. Inspired by the speech, students form "Americans Committed to World Responsibility" and organize a petition drive asking for the establishment of such a program; within weeks a thousand Michigan students have signed it.

January 20, 1961 President Kennedy includes what becomes basic Peace Corps philosophy in his inaugural address: "To those peoples in the huts and villages of half the globe struggling to break the bonds of mass misery, we pledge our best efforts to help them help themselves..."

January 21, 1961 President Kennedy appoints Sargent Shriver as head of a task force to study the feasibility of a Peace Corps. Shriver enlists the help of Harris Wofford. Together they draw up plans and invite suggestions from various quarters.

March 1, 1961 President Kennedy issues Executive Order creating Peace Corps. Three days later, Sargent Shriver is appointed its first director.

August 30, 1961 President Kennedy hosts ceremony at the White House Rose Garden in honor of the first group of Peace Corps Volunteers departing for service in Ghana.

September 22, 1961 Congress approves legislation formally authorizing Peace Corps with the mandate to "promote world peace and friendship" through the following objectives: (1) To help the people of interested countries and areas in meeting their needs for trained manpower; (2) To help promote a better understanding of Americans on the part of the peoples served; and, (3) To help promote a better understanding of other peoples on the part of Americans.

December 31, 1961 By the end of the year, Peace Corps programs start up in Brazil, Chile, Colombia, Ghana, India, Malaysia, Nigeria, Pakistan, Philippines, St. Lucia, Sierra Leone, Tanzania and Thailand. Total number of volunteers reaches 750.

1962 Programs begin in Afghanistan, Belize, Bolivia, Cameroon, Cyprus, Dominican Republic, Ecuador, El Salvador, Ethiopia, Iran, Ivory Coast, Jamaica, Liberia, Nepal, Niger, Peru, Somali Republic, Sri Lanka (Ceylon), Togo, Tunisia, Turkey and Venezuela. As of June 30, 1962, 2,816 volunteers are in the field.

1963 Programs begin in Costa Rica, Gabon, Grenada, Guatemala, Guinea, Honduras, Indonesia, Malawi, Morocco, Panama, Senegal and Uruguay. As of June 30, 1963, there are 6,646 volunteers in the field.

April 1964 Peace Corps Partnership Program is started to provide a link between U.S. contributors and requests for project assistance from the overseas communities in which Peace Corps Volunteers serve. March 5-7, 1965 First national Returned Volunteer Conference is held in Washington, D.C.

July 1, 1971 President Nixon creates the ACTION agency, to incorporate various federal voluntary organizations including Peace Corps, VISTA, Older Americans Programs, and other smaller programs.

1974 Peace Corps programs are operating in 69 countries. Programs begin in Bahrain, Seychelles and Tuvalu (Ellice Islands). As of June 30, there are 8,044 volunteers and trainees in the field.

November 1978 First returned Peace Corps volunteer is elected to U.S. Senate—Paul Tsongas, a volunteer in Ethiopia from 1962 to 1964.

April 27, 1979 President Carter signs amendment to ACTION legislation granting Peace Corps special independence. Richard Celeste is appointed Peace Corps director and ACTION associate director for International Operations.

October 14, 1980 Special 20th anniversary commemorative service is held at the Student Union at the University of Michigan in Ann Arbor.

March 1, 1981 President Reagan offers congratulations to Peace Corps on the 20th anniversary of Kennedy's executive order.

June 2, 1981 20th anniversary of returned Peace Corps Volunteers held in Washington, D.C. Peace Corps has had programs in 88 countries; 97,201 Americans have become Peace Corps volunteers and/or trainees.

February 22, 1982 Peace Corps is re-established as an independent agency.

January 30, 1985 The first Peace Corps Fellows Program is established at Teachers College/Columbia University to recruit, prepare and place RPCVs as teachers in the New York City public schools. In exchange for a two-year work commitment, the RPCVs are offered scholarships for graduate study.

October 6-7, 1985 Peace Corps begins its 25th anniversary year in Ann Arbor, at the University of Michigan with a two-day seminar on "America's Role in Africa's Development: Past and Future" that attracts leading scholars from Africa and the United States. Present for the event are Vice President Bush, Sargent Shriver and Jack Hood Vaughn.

September 19-20, 1986 Nearly 5,000 returned Peace Corps Volunteers gather at the Washington Mall to celebrate Peace Corps' 25th anniversary. More than 7,000 returned Peace Corps volunteers, staff, friends and their families walk from the Lincoln Memorial to Arlington Cemetery for memorial honoring 199 Peace Corps volunteers who died in service overseas.

November 20, 1988 The John F. Kennedy Library hosts a special Peace Corps remembrance of President Kennedy, 25 years after his death. At the event, Peace Corps archives, including voluminous volunteer journals and other artifacts, are formally donated to the Library.

November 22, 1988 Returned Volunteers across the country join together in celebration of President John F. Kennedy's "living legacy" on the 25th anniversary of his death. Several hundred former volunteers stage a 24-hour vigil at the Capitol Rotunda that ends with a memorial service at St. Matthew's Cathedral in Washington.

The Peace Corps Story

January 20, 1989 Carrying the flags of more than 60 nations where Peace Corps serves, a group of former volunteers and staff march for the first time ever in a presidential inaugural parade.

July 1989 President Bush announces from Budapest that Peace Corps volunteers will go to Hungary, establishing the first Peace Corps program in an Eastern European country.

September 28, 1989 Director Paul Coverdell announces Peace Corps' "World Wise Schools" initiative. This program matches Peace Corps volunteers overseas with elementary and junior high classes in the United States in an effort to promote international awareness and cross-cultural understanding. By the late fall of 1989 more than 550 schools were participating in the unique education program.

June 15, 1990 In a White House Rose Garden ceremony President Bush praises "the group of talented Americans who are...to take leave of these shores — and become the first Peace Corps volunteers to serve in Eastern Europe." The 121 volunteers will meet with the President during their stop over in Washington, D.C. en route to Poland and Hungary.

March 1, 1991 Peace Corps celebrates its 30th anniversary. President Bush signs a Congressional Resolution and Proclamation honoring Peace Corps' 30 years of service. More than 125,000 people have served in over 100 countries.

August 1-4, 1991 Peace Corps celebrates its 30th anniversary in Washington, D.C., with festivities on the mall for Returned Peace Corps Volunteers.

July 22, 1992 The first group of Peace Corps Volunteers leaves for the former Soviet Union. These Volunteers will work in small business enterprise projects in Lithuania, Estonia, and Latvia.

November 21, 1992 The first group of 100 business Volunteers leaves for Russia.

June 12, 1993 The first group of 18 English teacher Volunteers leaves for China.

October 7, 1993 The United States Senate confirms Carol Bellamy by unanimous consent to head the agency. Bellamy is the first Returned Peace Corps Volunteer to hold this position.

April 1994 Peace Corps Partnership program celebrates its 30th anniversary. Over the course of its 30 years, Peace Corps Partnership Program has supported nearly 3,500 volunteer projects in more than 80 developing countries.

January 30, 1995 Peace Corps Fellows program celebrates its 10th anniversary. Over 50,000 students have been taught by Peace Corps fellows.

August 11, 1995 The United States Senate confirms Mark D. Gearan, former Assistant to the President and Director of Communications and Strategic Planning, as the director of the agency.

SKILLS NEEDED FOR PEACE CORPS PROGRAMS

Agriculture:
Two or four year degree, or two to five years experience.

Agribusiness	Agronomy
Agriculture Education	Fisheries
Animal Husbandry	Crop Extension
Forestry	Soil Science
Parks and Wildlife Management	Environmental Education

Skilled Trades:
Vocational/Technical Education or Industrial Arts degree, or two to five years professional experience.

Carpentery	Auto or Deisel Mechanics
Construction	Electrical Work
Machining	Metal Working
Plumbing	Masonry

Professional Services
Two or four year degree, or two to five years experience:

Business Management	Road Construction Engineering
NGO Development	Water & Sanitation Engineering
Cooperatives	Hydrology
Nursing	Health Education
Nutrition	Social Work

Education
Bachelor's degree or appropriate certification; experience preferred but not always required.

English/TEFL	Math
Chemistry	Physics
Biology	Special Education
Primary Teacher Training	Secondary Teacher Training

HOW TO BECOME A COMPETITIVE CANDIDATE

Becoming a Peace Corps Volunteer today can be a challenge...but the right combination of work, education and volunteer experience can qualify you for an assignment. Following are the basic requirements for several programs which heavily weigh community and language skills. A minimum of three months experience in planning, organizing, counseling or leadership within the past four years, and in many cases a background in French or Spanish, can determine competitiveness.

If you're interested in:
English Teaching

You will need:
B.A./B.S. any discipline with 6 to 12 months of ESL tutoring experience within the past four years. The tutoring must be at least ten hours a month in a structured program that provides pre-service training. The student(s) should be at least 12 years of age.

Health & Nutrition Extension — B.A./B.S. any discipline with First Aid, EMT or CPR Certificates and/or 3 to 6 months health experience such as Planned Parenthood counseling or hospital/clinic or emergency room experience. LPNs with two years post-license experience are also competitive.

Agriculture & Forestry Extension — B.A./B.S. any discipline with 6 to 12 months experience in vegetable gardening, forestry, greenhouse, or nursery. Extensive leadership, organizing or initiative is often required beyond the required minimum. Many applicants have over 5 years gardening experience.

Public Health/Sanitation — B.A./B.S. any discipline with 3 to 6 months experience in construction, masonry, carpentry or plumbing. The most competitive applicants have experience working with concrete and building forms.

| *Community Services* | B.A./B.S. in any discipline with strong experience in planning, organizing, counseling or leadership within the past four years. The program is extremely competitive. Most current requests require additional experience such as: AIDS counseling, teaching, urban youth development, medical or mental health counseling. |

Some things to keep in mind...
- The above-mentioned experience is the minimum amount required or suggested. In all cases, the more the better. Remember, we cannot guarantee placement.

- For all Education assignments, the overall quality of the application (e.g., spelling and grammatical errors) is an important factor in selection.

- French or Spanish are required for many programs, and fluency in French, rather than a specific technical skill, can sometimes qualify an applicant for an assignment. Other factors being equal, applicants who have recently studied French, Spanish, Portuguese or any other language are more competitive than those who have not.

- Contact a Recruiter at your local Peace Corps office at (800) 424-8580 to discuss how your skills can best be used overseas.

THE APPLICATION PROCESS

Applying to the Peace Corps can be exciting, but it can also be challenging. The application process involves essays, interviews, letters of recommendation, and medical and dental examinations. This guide will familiarize you with the application screening and placement process.

Volunteer Projects

Peace Corps overseas programmers work closely with host-country agencies to develop projects and identify Volunteer assignments. Peace Corps recruitment offices then target their efforts toward identifying the best applicants for the skills needed by host countries.

Timing of Requests

Requests are grouped into four "seasons" according to when Volunteers report to pre-departure orientation prior to leaving the U.S. for their overseas assignment. The seasons are as follows:

Fall:	October - December
Winter:	January - March
Spring:	April - June
Summer:	July - September

The recruitment and placement process begins up to 9 months prior to the beginning of a season. For example, a Volunteer who begins training during the spring season will likely have begun the application process during the previous fall. Couples may take up to 12 months.

More than two candidates are identified for each Volunteer requested; thus, the selection process is competitive. There are four major steps in the application process. Each step is described in the sections that follow.

- ◆ Application
- ◆ Nomination
- ◆ Qualification
- ◆ Invitation

Step I: Application

Applications Are Reviewed

Upon receiving your application, your recruitment office will send you a confirmation of receipt letter. Your Recruiter will then review your application to determine if your skills and interests match those requested by Peace Corps programs overseas.

All requests for Volunteers are grouped into 44 assignment areas in six programming categories:

- ◆ Environment
- ◆ Agriculture
- ◆ Health
- ◆ Community Development
- ◆ Business and Skilled Trades
- ◆ Education

If you meet the requirements for any of the assignment areas for which Volunteers have been requested, you will be contacted by your Recruiter to schedule an interview.

Your application may be withdrawn from further consideration for any of the following reasons:

- You are not a U.S. citizen
- You are under 18 years old
- You are under supervised probation
- You are or have been involved in intelligence organizations
- You have dependents
- Your particular skills do not match those requested by Peace Corps host countries

Applicants Are Interviewed

The interview with your Recruiter usually takes place within a month of receipt of your application. Most applicants are interviewed in person; others may arrange interviews by phone. During the interview your Recruiter will explore your flexibility, adaptability, social sensitivity, cultural awareness, motivation, and commitment to Peace Corps service. Your Recruiter will not nominate you to an assignment area without an expression of genuine commitment on your part to Peace Corps service.

In addition to meeting the requirements for an assignment area and completing the interview, there must be a current opening for Volunteers with your skills and experience at the time you are available for Peace Corps service. If there is a request, you will then compete with candidates with similar skills applying to the same recruitment office.

If you are chosen to fill a current opening, you will be "nominated" by your Recruiter for a specific assignment area. A nomination means that your Recruiter formally places your name into consideration for one of many requests for Volunteers with your skills and experience. You must still compete with nominees from other recruitment offices around the country for specific country assignments.

Things To Do During The Application Phase

- Submit the application, the Report of Medical History form, a copy of your transcripts, and two copies of your résumé to the local recruitment office.

- Respond to the request to schedule an interview as soon as possible.
- Keep copies of all application materials.

Step 2: Nomination

Applicants Are Nominated

If you are nominated to an assignment area, your Recruiter will notify you by mail and provide you with your assignment area number and title, and the season of departure (e.g., AA100 Forestry, Spring 1996).

Along with the letter confirming your nomination, your "nomination kit" will contain reference forms and envelopes, an update questionnaire, and forms for completing fingerprints and the applicant background investigation. Please review the materials carefully and contact your Recruiter if you have any questions. All forms must be completed promptly and forwarded to the Evaluation Division in Washington D.C. in the envelope provided.

At the time you are nominated, your Recruiter may be able to tell you the geographic region (i.e., Africa, Asia-Pacific, Inter-America, or Europe/Central Asia/Mediterranean) of the assignment, but will not be able to tell you the specific country. Specific country assignments are determined during the invitation phase of the application process.

References

In order to fully assess your qualifications for Peace Corps service, you will be required to submit four references, one each from the following categories:

- current/most recent work supervisor
- volunteer supervisor
- professor, advisor, or counselor
- personal acquaintance or co-worker

Mail or hand-deliver the reference forms to your references as soon as possible. Stress the importance of completing the forms thoroughly and returning them to you sealed and signed across the back of the envelope. Once you have collected all four references, you will forward them to the Evaluation Division. Please contact the Evaluation Division if you are having difficulties.

Fingerprint/Background Check

All applicants are required to submit to a thorough background investigation as part of the application process. Fingerprints may be done at the local Peace Corps recruitment office at the time of your interview or after you have been nominated. Many police stations and state Divisions of Motor Vehicles (DMV) will also fingerprint applicants, but may charge a small fee.

Things To Do During The Nomination Phase

- Contact references and urge them to complete the reference form as soon as possible.
- Complete the fingerprint and background investigation forms.
- Complete the update questionnaire.
- Mail all four references, fingerprints and background investigation forms, and the update questionnaire to the Evaluation Division within 30 days of receipt of your nomination kit.

Step 3: Qualification

Applicants Are Evaluated

Once you are nominated, the recruitment office will forward your application and a summary of your interview to the Evaluation Division. During the qualification phase, your Evaluator will review your application, references, and other supporting documents to verify that your technical skills and experience match those needed for the assignment. Your Evaluator will also assess your suitability for Volunteer service using motivation, commitment, emotional maturity, social sensitivity, and cultural awareness as assessment criteria.

Medical History Is Reviewed

Your Recruiter will forward your sealed medical package to the Office of Medical Services (OMS) as soon as you are nominated. A member of the OMS medical screening team will review your completed Medical History form as soon as it arrives in OMS. A medical examination packet will then be mailed to most applicants. A very small number of applicants may be deferred or medically disqualified from Peace Corps service based on information in their Medical History form. All applicants who receive the medical examination packet must undergo physical and dental examinations using the forms in the packet.

The results of the medical and dental examinations must be reviewed by OMS before an applicant can receive medical and dental clearance. It is your responsibility to provide all information required to determine your medical suitability for Volunteer service. Medical and dental processing time can be shortened by submitting complete and thorough information as quickly as possible. When known, please include the dates of events or conditions.

Medical and dental problems which could hinder your performance as a Volunteer must be resolved before you can be invited to serve in a specific assignment and country. Peace Corps will reimburse the cost of medical and dental examinations up to prescribed limits based on age, gender, and other factors; however, Peace Corps cannot pay for corrective health procedures or for special evaluations.

Legal Information Is Reviewed

Only applicants who meet the legal standards of eligibility established by Congress and Peace Corps may be invited to enter pre-service training for a Volunteer assignment. If any of the legal issues listed below apply to you, your application will be reviewed by the Legal Liaison in the Office of Placement. Please note that the following circumstances do not necessarily disqualify you from Peace Corps service but will require clarification and documentation before the Legal Liaison can make a determination of your eligibility for Volunteer service:

◆ common law marriage
◆ married, serving without spouse
◆ divorce
◆ dependents
◆ previous convictions
◆ student loans
◆ financial obligations (e.g., home mortgage payments, child support)
◆ bankruptcy
◆ association with intelligence activity
◆ current obligations to the military

Nominees Are Qualified

If you meet the skill requirements and suitability assessment criteria for Volunteer service, you will receive a letter from the Evaluation Division notifying you that you have been qualified and that your file has been forwarded to the appropriate Skill Desk.

The qualification process generally takes five to eight weeks from the date of nomination. If you have not submitted your four references, your fingerprints are illegible, or your application has been placed on hold for medical or legal reasons, the qualification process may be delayed.

Things To Do During The Qualification Phase

◆ Complete the medical and dental examinations as soon as possible.
◆ Respond to all requests for additional medical, legal, and other information.
◆ Contact the Evaluation Division at (800) 424-8580, ext. 2218 or (202) 606-2080 in the Washington, D.C. area if there are changes in your address, phone number, or other relevant information.

Step 4: Invitation

Applicants Are Invited

When your application reaches the Skill Desk, your Placement Officer will assess your application against country-specific criteria.

Placement Officers make the final decision whether to invite an applicant to begin pre-service training. The placement process is competitive and is designed to ensure that Peace Corps Volunteers have not only the technical skills needed, but also the personal qualities necessary to work successfully in a specific assignment.

If you receive an invitation, you will have 10 days from the mailing date of the invitation letter to respond. The invitation packet also includes a Volunteer Assignment Description (VAD) to help you make the decision whether to accept the invitation, passport and visa applications, a pre-training questionnaire, and an invitation booklet to guide you in preparing for departure.

If you have not heard from your Placement Officer 30 days after you receive your qualification letter from the Evaluation Division, you should call the appropriate Skill Desk to check the status of your application.

Once you have accepted an invitation, Peace Corps will send you additional information to help you prepare for departure. The Country Desk Officer for your country of assignment will send you a packet of information about your host country and a description of your pre-service training. The packet will include a recommended clothing list and a country-specific bibliography.

Approximately 4 weeks prior to departure, you will receive reporting instructions with the date and location of your pre-departure orientation. The Travel Office will send you airline tickets and soon you will be on your way!

Things To Do During The Invitation Phase
- Respond to the invitation within 10 days.
- Contact the appropriate Skill Desk at (800) 424-8580 if there are changes in your address, phone number, availability date, or other relevant information.

ACTIVE PEACE CORPS COUNTRIES
(As of September, 1996)

Africa
Benin
Botswana
Burkina Faso
Cameroon
Cape Verde
Central Africa Republic
Chad
Congo
Côte d'Ivoire
Eritrea
Ethiopia
Gabon
The Gambia
Ghana
Guinea
Guinea Bissau
Kenya
Lesotho
Madagascar
Mali
Malawi
Mauritania
Namibia
Niger
Senegal
South Africa
Swaziland
Tanzania
Togo
Uganda
Zambia
Zimbabwe

The Americas
Belize
Bolivia
Chile
Costa Rica
Dominican Republic
Eastern Caribbean
- ◆ Antigua/Barbuda
- ◆ Dominica
- ◆ Grenada
- ◆ Montserrat
- ◆ St. Kitts/Nevis
- ◆ St. Lucia
- ◆ St. Vincent & Grenadines
Ecuador

El Salvador
Guatemala
Guyana
Haiti
Honduras
Jamaica
Nicaragua
Panama
Paraguay
Suriname
Uruguay

Asia and the Pacific
China
Fiji
Kiribati
Micronesia
Mongolia
Nepal
Niue
Palau
Papua New Guinea
Philippines
Solomon Islands
Sri Lanka
Thailand
Tonga
Tuvalu
Vanuatu
Western Samoa

Europe, Central Asia, and the Mediterranean
Albania
Armenia
Bulgaria
Czech Republic
Estonia
Hungary
Kazakhstan
Kyrghystan
Latvia
Lithuania
Malta
Moldova
Morocco
Poland
Romania
Russia
Slovakia
Turkmenistan
Ukraine
Uzbekistan

Former Peace Corps Countries

Africa
Burundi
Comoros
Equatorial Guinea
Liberia
Nigeria
Rwanda
Seychelles
Sao Tomé & Principe
Sierra Leone
Somalia
Sudan
Zaire

The Americas
Anguilla
Argentina
Barbados
Brazil
Colombia
Peru
Turks & Caicos
Venezuela

Asia and Pacific
Bangladesh
Cook Islands
India
Indonesia
Malaysia
Marshall Islands
Mauritius
Pakistan
South Korea

Europe, Central Asia, and the Mediterranean
Afghanistan
Bahrain
Cyprus
Iran
Israel
Libya
Oman
Tunisia
Turkey
Yemen